Unlocking the Secrets of Jesus' Stories

Pierre F. Steenberg, Ph.D., D.Min.

Copyright © 2012 Pierre F. Steenberg, Ph.D., D.Min.

Email: Pierre@Steenberg.US

All rights reserved.

ISBN-10: 1463664125
ISBN-13: 978-1463664121

Printed in the United States of America

DEDICATION

I dedicate this work to my wife:
She is my best friend
Her support is unsurpassed
Her love is unfailing
Her laughter is contagious
She is the love of my life.

CONTENTS

ACKNOWLEDGMENTS

The character of the book was shaped by various theological professors, who guided my academic endeavors for many years. I wish to express a great deal of gratitude to the churches where I have had the privilege of "pastoring". They have endured listening to me, developing the contents of this book from sermon to sermon. The same is true for camp meetings, where I was invited as a guest speaker in California, as well as in South Africa.

PART I: Tools for Unlocking the Secrets of Jesus' Stories

Pierre F. Steenberg, Ph.D., D.Min.

⚜ CHAPTER ONE ⚜

INTRODUCTION

When a traditional Zulu receives a gift, both his hands are extended to accept it, the one behind the other. This is to express honesty and that nothing is hidden in the other hand; it is a sign of respect. Yet, when a non-Zulu donates a gift, the Zulu's action of extending both hands to accept it may be interpreted as greed, signifying the desire for more.

When two traditional Zulus observe one another walking on opposite sides of a busy street, they will loudly greet each other and continue their conversation above the traffic noise. Non-Zulus walking past them may think this behavior is rude and unacceptable, as they could rather go toward each other to have a normal conversation, rather than shouting their private business for all to overhear. Zulu people are quite comfortable talking this way as it demonstrates that they have nothing to hide. When Zulus see people standing close to each other, speaking so that others cannot hear their conversation, it creates suspicion, as they might discuss something secretly.

Assuming traditional gender roles when guests visit our homes, the lady of the house would enter the kitchen to prepare something to drink. Returning with a heavy tray, the man of the house would jump up to assist her. If he would not do this he would be regarded as rude. In the Zulu home, however, it would be believed to be rude for the man to assist, for he is depriving her of the opportunity to be a good housewife. One might notice the confusion when two dissimilar families would get together for a visit. The "non-Zulu" would think that the Zulu is rude when he would not assist his wife, and so the "non-Zulu" would get up to support her; if he would do this, however, the Zulu would consider him to be impolite for not allowing his wife to be the woman of the house. It was a rich experience to grow up with many Zulu people and my father spoke Zulu well.

While attending orientation meetings in Kenya prior to preaching engagements we were taught not to use our right hands, but rather only our left hands, when making gestures.

English teachers who served in South Korea were quickly taught not to blow their noses in public. One day, after conducting an Indian wedding, I invited the marriage couple to kiss each other. The bride and the groom, however, looked at me in horror. Their happy facial expressions turned into big question marks. Both asked simultaneously, "In front of everyone?" Later I found out that this was unacceptable in the Indian culture.

All of the above cultural examples would make no sense to a person from another culture who did not share at least some knowledge of that particular culture. To comprehend what is happening, an outsider has to be well-informed about the habits functioning in the insider's group, and how behavior is supposed to be perceived. The outsider has to be equipped with skills to understand the cultural customs, or else misunderstanding and misinterpretation results.

Imagine with me, if you would, that you are single and available for a relationship. You are on vacation in a distant country. A potential person who may become a friend catches your eye. You walk over to meet this person, only to realize that neither of you speak any languages in common. What's more, you do not know what is culturally acceptable and what is considered presumptuous with regards to making any advances. What is needed for this relationship to be initiated? Probably one of you would have to learn the other's language. In addition you would have to study the culture and customs of the other person, and vice versa. Learning the other person's language is a skill that you could use to get to know the other person. Probably, without these tools an authentic relationship would not be established.

Now, we face the same problems with understanding the "stories" of the New Testament. We have to understand that the New Testament also belongs to a different culture of a different time and from a different country, with different customs.

If we wish to understand these New Testament events we have to understand their contexts. In order to understand New Testament events and people we have to equip ourselves with the tools and skills necessary to do so. Without these indispensable keys that unlock their culture and customs we automatically interpret what we read in the context of our own culture.

The problem and challenge is that the New Testament "stories" did not take place in our culture, or in our context. The consequences would be that when we read New Testament "stories" we would miss their sense and meaning completely. To unlock the secrets of the New Testament we have to be familiar with its culture, thinking, mindset, and context. The issue is not what certain New Testament passages would mean to us, but rather, what those passages would have meant to the original New Testament readers. Once we have a good idea how they could have seen the text we could apply the same principles of meaning in our context.

Pierre F. Steenberg, Ph.D., D.Min.

❧ CHAPTER TWO ☙

THE IMPORTANCE OF CONTEXT

A great deal has been said and written about the importance of understanding the context of Biblical passages.[1]

This means to most people, however, that *we should not interpret texts out of context.* The idea is that the text is to be read within the context of the story in which it appears: The text about our bodies being a temple of God, for example, is often used to support the topic of health.

> *Or do you not know that your body is a temple of the Holy Spirit in you, whom you have of God? And you are not your own, for you are bought with a price. Therefore glorify God in your body and in your spirit, which are God's (1 Cor 6: 19-20).*

The context of this text actually refers to sexual purity and does not point to dietary guidance. Using the text to say what it does not really mean within the context of the entire passage, is exploiting and abusing the text out of context.

Defining "context" in this way, while important, is rather a limiting view of the term. There is also the more comprehensive and often unnoticed and disregarded context of a person's mindset, the culture, social rules and customs of the day: There is the written context

---

[1] Context is crucial when it comes to understanding the New Testament (Longenecker 2009, 422).

referring to the actual context written down in the story, and there is also the unwritten or unrecorded context.

It is this unwritten context that is just as important as the written context, which causes such a great deal of misinterpretation. This kind of context was not a "written-down" context as it was known and shared amongst the people in the society in which the story was written down. One simply takes it for granted that this has been common knowledge and, therefore, it was not necessary to be written down.

Every sport, for example, has unwritten rules: A golfer is not supposed to step into the pathway between the other player's ball and the hole. This "regulation" is not written down as a rule, yet all golf players know about it and practices this courtesy.

If golf would stop being played today and someone would discover golf videos a thousand years from now, they would not understand why a golfer got upset with a friend for stepping onto the pathway between his ball and the hole. They might go to the museum to look at an ancient golf rule book, but that would not shed any light on the matter as the rule was never written down.

If we look at a newspaper article on sport, we notice the same thing. The article assumes that the reader knows the sport and its vocabulary. The article does not explain what a curve ball is, or what RBI stands for. The paper assumed correctly that people reading the article know baseball. People who read about baseball or golf share common knowledge about the sport. A person, who has never heard about golf and looks at a newspaper headline, thinking that golf is about shots being taken at birdies and eagles, may be forgiven.

Similarly, every society has a common, shared context; it is those aspects society agrees upon and that provide meaning to communication. These aspects of the context are often disregarded, as they are taken for granted. They are not explained, or known by most modern Bible readers. It is exactly these specific aspects of the context, however, that provide a face to the faceless, and emotion and cognition to descriptions or names, and societal interaction and communication to those people and entities, which are apparently detached.

The people in the past have lived to a great extent as we live in terms of being real people with real relational issues and societal difficulties. They lived and existed in a context. We would not understand their lives and stories entirely without our comprehension of their general and broader context.

It is important to realize that *context determines meaning:* If the word "canon", for example, was the only word mentioned, what would you think about? Military personnel may conclude that it referred to a cannon, shooting cannon balls. Photographers may be forgiven if they think that the word refers to a camera brand. Biblical scholars may think that the concept refers to the 66 books of the Bible.

Intrinsically, *words have no meaning,* as this example demonstrates; on the contrary, *meanings have words.*[2] Meaning is contextually derived and determined. The meaning of words, therefore, can only be understood if they are substantiated in the context within which they appear.

The concept of "context" for our purposes actually refers to three different types of contexts or frameworks, which influence meaning and understanding:

Firstly, there is the written context of *the story.*

Secondly, there is the unwritten or unrecorded context of *the society* in which the story was penned: Society's habits, world views, interactions, communications, collaborations, protocols, manners, etc.

Lastly, there is the context of *the readers,* which also influences their interpretation of what is read, based upon their unarticulated and unwritten context.

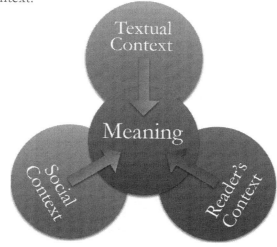

---

[2] The statement, "meaning having words", comes from Prof. J. van der Watt, former Dean of the New Testament Faculty at the University of Pretoria.

As far as possible, *our goal is to recreate the generalized unwritten context in which the story has been written.* As we seek to understand the New Testament stories we also have to endeavor to understand and comprehend the context of the New Testament:

Without understanding its context, the New Testament only informs us of "faceless people", without backgrounds and environments, which seem to be characters on paper only.

Without understanding the social context, the modern reader often does not understand the people in the story, nor their interactions, backgrounds and communication.

The people in the New Testament were real people with content and environmental substance. They experienced real emotions, moods and sentiments. In addition, they did not function merely as individuals, without contact with others. They formed liaisons and groups, just as today. They had families and relationships. Relationships were governed by mutually-agreed upon and known paradigms and frameworks. When people interacted with each other, these paradigms were presupposed, not explained. They were not even mentioned and they were not elucidated or explained, as they were clearly and automatically accepted and commonly shared among everybody.

The trouble starts when people do not share a given paradigm or common framework: Readers who are from a different time, or from another culture, or from a dissimilar paradigm, attempt to understand communication located within the unknown and unshared paradigm and framework. This is the reason why it is automatically assumed that the word "cannon" refer to a military weapon, as this is the contemporary context in which they find themselves. Similarly, the current context of photography places upon "canon" the meaning of a brand name.

Yet, biblical scholars take this same word and apply a totally different meaning to it: The chosen meaning was based upon the context of the interpreter. When reading New Testament stories we often interpret them, based upon our present-day context rather than that of the New Testament. This will lead to invalid interpretation. In fact, we may misunderstand the New Testament completely.

The conversation gets interesting, for example, when military personnel, the photographer and the biblical scholar meet. They use the same word or concept, but refer to different meanings. Each person understands the spoken word, "canon", based upon their own context, and they think mistakenly that they have understood what was meant. They are dreadfully mistaken, however, and misinterpret the meaning totally.

This misinterpretation happened because the same word was used in a different context from that of the listeners, and, consequently, referred to a different meaning. To avoid misinterpretation in such meetings, we determine meaning by way of the context of the conversation.

We also use "body language" to assist determining meaning: The general may use his hands to show something shooting or exploding, the photographer may demonstrate shooting with his finger on an imaginary camera, while the biblical scholar may open his hands in the form of a book. When we look at the body language it is clear what the speaker means when the word "canon" or "cannon" is used.

Things, however, may get more difficult now as both the general and the photographer use a "second word", referring to their two different events. To the general "to shoot" means to fire a weapon. To the photographer it means to take a picture with a camera. For a common understanding, either the general or the photographer needs to let go of their personal context and position their minds in the context of the other meaning.

In a similar way, understanding New Testament stories can only be achieved if we release our own contexts as much as possible, and assume the context of the New Testament, as much as is known.

Placing ourselves in another context sounds easy and, in fact, we do this all the time. It can only be done, however, if we understand the other context in which we place ourselves. I can place myself in the Zulu context as I understand it. I cannot place myself in the Polish context, however, as I have no knowledge of that context.

This is the real problem: We do not understand the context of the New Testament. As indicated, New Testament people shared and understood their context and, consequently, it was not necessary to explain it. People who explain the obvious seem foolish – it is just not done.

To a great extent interaction is governed by unwritten rules. These rules are simply assumed and seldom discussed. This means that we do not have some ancient book that explains the thinking of New Testament people. There is no place where we can find out what these people thought, how they were motivated, or in what way their interaction and communication worked.

The Bible, for example, does not explain anywhere the Judaic concept of time. We can simply read the New Testament and make our own assumptions, deductions and conclusions. We can also study other non-canonical or apocryphal writings of that time in an attempt to reconstruct the cultural context of New Testament people.

This is actually more difficult than it may seem, as all people in the New Testament era did not belong to the same group and to only one context. There were people, just as today, from all walks of life, and from all kinds of contexts, languages, cultures, education, and so forth.

Usually each group functions differently. The cultural rules and experiences of a gang, for example, are vastly different from those of a symphony orchestra. Similarly, the rules of interaction in a prison are vastly different from those in a school, a church, or a tennis club. For that reason it is not possible to reconstruct the cultural context for every possible group. There are simply too many groups and there is not enough information on each one of them. *In contrast we will deal with what most groups had in common.* A general view, therefore, is unavoidable and exceptions may abound.

Before we look at the New Testament stories themselves, we will combine some building blocks and constructions of the unwritten New Testament context, to use these combinations as tools to unlock the secrets of Jesus' New Testament stories.

❧ CHAPTER THREE ❧

TOOL I: GROUP ORIENTATION[3]

Today, people are evaluated on performance. Most people at work have annual reviews of performance. Everything is based upon achievement. Moreover, most importantly, a person is judged as an individual. In fact, most people in contemporary society use a couple of things to determine someone's value or standing in society:

- First they look at people's employment – performance. Doctors, engineers and other professionals are highly esteemed.
- Second, they look at other people's opinion of them - reputation.
- Finally, they look at what people own. If people possess large homes, expensive cars, luxury items and so forth, they often equate these assets with success and thereby, arrive at the conclusion that not only must they be successful, but they must be significant people too.

By the way, Christians are not to derive self-worth from performance, reputation and possessions. We derive our worth from what God thinks of us and from the extent of His love for us. *Be as it may, we look at ourselves as individuals.*

---

[3] Resources with regard to New Testament group orientation are: Malina 1993, 63-89; Malina and Neyrey 1991, 61-96; Malina and Neyrey 1996, 154-176; Hellerman 2000.

If someone is interviewed for a new position at work, his or her *curriculum vitae* or résumé is an important key to obtain the job. That résumé typically states information about the individual's achievements and skills. The person's résumé will list his or her qualifications and degrees; it will also provide a list of previous work experience. As can be seen from this example the information used to determine a person's value to a company is based solely on the individual's past performance and on the interview of the person.

In today's society people also belong to groups, but these groups have to do with activities, beliefs or friendships. Even within these groups we still regard ourselves as individuals. We do not wish to look like everybody else; in fact, if a woman attends a function and observes that another woman wears the same dress, there is pandemonium. If somebody appears differently, thinks otherwise, or behaves differently from the rest of us, we simply tolerate it, subject to certain boundaries within which they fall. In our society these boundaries are very wide indeed. Actually, our society encourages individuality in many cases.

In the time of the New Testament these boundaries were very narrow indeed. Social behavior was geared to keep people within specific boundaries, or to expel them if they stepped outside of them[4]. The people of the New Testament were group-oriented[5]. The group was more important than individuals. Individuals did what was best for the group. The group rewarded and punished its members into conformity.

Actually, in the time of the New Testament people were not looked upon as individuals[6], but rather as a part of a group,[7] or of multiple groups. Everyone belonged to a group[8]; people were born into a group. The choice of groups to belong to was not based upon activities, beliefs or friendships. Instead, it was based upon the status of the group. Each group was viewed narrowly in a stereotypical way. Personal views, beliefs or behavior which did not fit into these constricted boundaries resulted in social punishment, or expulsion from the group. A person's value system was defined by the group's value

---

[4] Malina 2002:6.
[5] Hagdorn and Neyrey 1998:20.
[6] Steenberg 2000:149-150; May 1997:207.
[7] Esler 2000:328.
[8] Malina 1996:35.

system[9]. Each group had a specific status and the group as a whole attempted to gain more status. A person who lost status in the eyes of the group was ostracized[10], socially punished and if the loss was significant enough, expelled.

If people were interviewed for positions at work during these times their résumés would read very differently from those of today. That résumé would not contain information about personal achievements or skills. It would not even list a person's qualifications or degrees. The résumé would not provide information about previous work experience. In fact, the entire interview would have nothing to do with the person as an individual, but rather with the group the applicant belonged to. A typical résumé would begin with a genealogy specifically designed to show the status ascribed to his or her group. If the interviewee was well educated, it was more important to state *who* educated the person in question. Even here the importance of the person who educated the applicant was not based upon the teacher's individual abilities or knowledge, but rather determined by the status of that person. In this case, the applicant's status would be similar to that of the teacher.

Paul was continually questioned as an apostle, especially in the Corinthian church. To persuade them, he presented his résumé:

> *Acts 22:3 I am truly a man, a Jew born in Tarsus in Cilicia, yet brought up in this city at the feet of Gamaliel, taught according to the exactness of the Law of the fathers, being a zealous one of God, as you all are today.*

Observe how Paul defined the group he belonged to:
- Firstly, he stated that he was a Jew. He also proved this by speaking the Hebrew dialect according to verse two.
- Secondly, he narrowed down his Jewish heritage to Tarsus.
- Thirdly, he named the person who educated him. The reason is that Gamaliel had an excellent status. By associating himself

---

[9] Neyrey 1998:27.
[10] Ostracism is mentioned as the main means of enforcing compliance and this most often resulted because of envy. Hagerdorn and Neyrey 1998:32.

with Gamaliel, he also identified himself with Gamaliel's honor. We know this as Gamaliel seemed to be highly honored.

Acts 5:34   Then there stood up one in the Sanhedrin, a Pharisee named Gamaliel, a doctor of the Law honored among all the people. And he commanded the apostles to be taken out for a while.

Towns also had a certain level of honor ascribed to them. In those days neighborhoods differed greatly from those of today. People did not associate with others of a lesser status. If that happened they would be degraded to the lower level. This indicated that all people from a particular neighborhood had the same honor or the same dishonor. The neighborhood became known, therefore, for that particular level of honor. Nazareth as an example is looked upon with little honor…

John 1:46   And Nathanael said to him, Can there be any good thing come out of Nazareth? Philip said to him, Come and see.

There were many similar signifiers of status groups, for example, place of origin, tribe, sect affiliation, and so forth. Another group signifying status was the family unit. When a person was born into a family, he or she automatically assumed the status of the family. This was the reason why New Testament stories almost always mentioned to which family a person belonged, or from which group they came. The New Testament, for example, did not only refer to John, but to John, son of Zebedee. Jesus was referred to as Jesus of Nazareth; or we read about Joseph of Arimathea. When a person was introduced in the New Testament the author would have almost always stated to which group the person belonged, for example, the Pharisees, Sadducees, Zealots, or the Sanhedrin.

We read about a fellow named Bartholomew (Matt 10:3); the word *"bar"* simply means "son of". So, here we have an individual whose individuality is of so little importance that he does not even have a name as his name literally means, son of Tolmai. Bartholomew is by no means an exception; there are well over 50 people in the New Testament alone who bear this type of name. For our purposes here three names will suffice: Barjona (Matt 16:17), Zacharias son of Barachias (Matt 23:35) and Barabbas (Matt 27:16).

The New Testament often mentioned the name of the tribe, to which people belonged, especially if they were from the royal tribe of David, or the tribe of Benjamin.

Every group was placed somewhere on a lineage of honor, vertically prioritized[11]. The groups with a great deal of honor had no dealings with any groups below them. Lower groups always attempted to associate with higher groups. If someone from a higher group associated with somebody from a lower group, the higher person's status diminished and the lower person's status increased. Such attempts to associate were also risky. If the higher person would reject the lower person's invitation of association, the lower person's status would drop.

Luke 14:12 And He also said to him who invited Him, When you make a dinner or a supper, do not call your friends or your brothers, or your kinsmen, or your rich neighbors; lest they also invite you again, and a recompense be made to you.

It was not proper to invite people with a higher status to functions. Here Jesus warned not to do this only to be invited again. The reason why Jesus said this was because people were not invited just to have a good time; they were invited to bolster the host's own status. The idea was to be invited again to establish a reciprocal relationship with the purpose of enhancing one's status. Usually such invitations would be publically rejected. People refused to associate with people below them. Jews who were considered to have a higher status than Samaritans[12] were not supposed to interact with them. Similarly, interaction between groups or individuals from different levels of status did not associate with each other, or when they did so, the association was frowned upon.

John 4:9 Then the woman of Samaria said to Him, How do you, being a Jew, ask a drink of me, who am a woman of Samaria? For the Jews do not associate with Samaritans.

---

[11] When individuals and groups are ranked in a society, such societies are called stratified societies (Chance 1994:141).
[12] Esler 2000:330.

Acts 11:2-3 And when Peter had come up to Jerusalem, those of the circumcision contended with him, saying, you went in to uncircumcised men and ate with them.

Matt 9:11 And when the Pharisees saw, they said to His disciples, Why does your master eat with tax-collectors and sinners?

Luke 5:30 But their scribes and Pharisees murmured against His disciples, saying, Why do you eat and drink with tax-collectors and sinners?

When Jesus associated with lower classes, those from the higher classes could not understand this; it did not make sense to them. Consequently, the only possible conclusion with their traditional way of thinking was that Jesus associated with them because He was one of them - He shared their status. Thus, we find the following accusations leveled against Him:

Luke 7:34 The Son of Man has come eating and drinking, and you say, Behold a gluttonous man and a winebibber, a friend of tax-collectors and sinners!

This is Jesus speaking; so, obviously He was aware of their opinion of him.

The highest honor was found high up on the vertical status line, while lower status was found lower down on the status line. Somewhere near the bottom of this line society drew a horizontal line. Anybody falling below this line was deemed unacceptable. The name assigned to people falling below this line was "sinner." When someone or a group was called a sinner or sinners in the Gospels it did not mean that they were sinners due to any particular sin that they committed. The word "sinner" was a status term referring to those who were socially rejected and deemed unacceptable. Lepers, the sick, the disabled, illegitimate children, prostitutes, tax-collectors,[13] and so forth, belonged to this category.

---

[13] Friedrichsen 2005:112.

People did all they could to climb up the status ladder. They also refused to do anything that would drop their status down to a lower level. Once people fell beneath the horizontal status line they were rejected by everyone above the line.

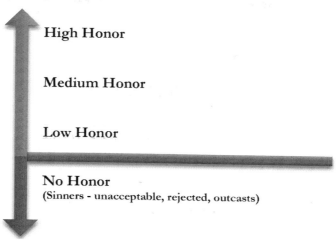

High Honor

Medium Honor

Low Honor

No Honor
(Sinners - unacceptable, rejected, outcasts)

In Matthew 13 Jesus was preaching in the synagogue. The audience was utterly impressed with what Jesus said. By their own admission they stated that Jesus was wise. In a performance-based society Jesus would have been lauded as a great orator on this occasion. Nonetheless, the unthinkable happened: Someone identified the group to which Jesus belonged, and since Jesus' particular group was of low honor, He had to be of low honor too. They now promptly rejected Jesus regardless of how highly they thought of Him prior to the disclosure of His status group. Consequently, His personal behavior or performance was irrelevant to this society. The group to which a person belongs to undermines individuality or personal performance in determining someone's value or status. All the impressive things Jesus did and just preached about were rejected simply because of the group to which Jesus belonged.

Matt 13:54-57 And when He had come into His own country, He taught them in their synagogue, so much so that they were astonished and said, From where does this man have this wisdom and these mighty works? Is not this the carpenter's son? Is not his mother called Mary? And his brothers, James and Joses and Simon and Judas, and his sisters, are they not all with us? Then from where does this man have all these things? And they were offended in Him. But Jesus said to them, A prophet is not without honor, except in his own country and in his own house.

It was just amazing that they could swing from astonishment to being offended so quickly. Jesus' rejection based on the group, which He came from, was so strong that they felt offended by Him. The reason why they reacted so strongly was because they listened to Him, which implied adherence to Him. This implied relationship meant that the listener's status would be influenced by the speaker's status. Since the speaker's status was just disclosed to be next to nothing it also meant an immense decrease in status to the listeners. They were upset as their status was largely reduced. Perhaps, based on what Jesus said, they expected Him to be some esteemed Teacher. They expected their status to be upgraded because of their association with this esteemed Teacher; only to find out that Jesus was a "nobody" in society's sight. Instead of having their status increased as expected, they now found their status reduced. They must have been shocked enormously; what a letdown! No wonder they were angry.

Here are a few more examples of people or groups who were deemed to have little or no honor:

Mat 9:10 And it happened as Jesus reclined in the house, behold, many tax-collectors and sinners came and were reclining with Him and His disciples.

Luke 7:39 But seeing this, the Pharisee who had invited Him, spoke within himself, saying, This man, if he were a prophet, would have known who and what kind of woman this is who touches him, for she is a sinner.

Luke 13:2 And answering, Jesus said to them, Do you suppose that these Galileans were sinners above all the Galileans because they suffered such things?

People generally believed that the tragedy of the tower falling on them that left eighteen dead was an act of God to punish them because they were sinners. People accepted that people who fall below the line of acceptance were punished by God. Society at large, therefore, also punished them, thereby assisting God to execute his judgment. If a person dared to help a sinner, it was considered an act against God. Harsh treatment of people with no honor was seen as doing God a favor – to help punish them. Here is a statement from Jesus explaining the sentiment that when people persecute others they do so because they believe that they are doing God a favor:

John 16:2 They shall put you out of the synagogue. But an hour is coming that everyone who kills you will think that he bears God service.

There are many examples of people in the New Testament looking down on those with a lower status. Here, only one example will be mentioned:

Luke 18:11-13 The Pharisee stood and prayed within himself in this way: God, I thank You that I am not as other men are, extortioners, unjust, adulterers, or even like this tax-collector. I fast twice on the Sabbath, I give tithes of all that I possess. And standing afar off, the tax-collector would not even lift up his eyes to Heaven, but struck on his breast, saying, God be merciful to me a sinner!

Note here the contrast between the highly honored Pharisee and the lowly tax collector.[14] Notice also that the tax collector literally stood far off; the Pharisee would not allow him to come close for fear of being associated with him and thereby dragging down his status. Being sick or disabled was seen as evidence of wrongdoing and, consequently, a low status or no status at all. Even after a person was healed it was still difficult not to view that person as a sinner.

John 9:24 Then a second time they called the man who was blind and said to him, give glory to God. We know that this man is a sinner.

---

[14] Friedrichsen 2005:95.

This man was deemed a sinner simply because of his blindness. This made perfect sense to the mindset of the people of the New Testament times as they thought that the man was blind because of his sinful status. Even Jesus' disciples subscribed to this view:

John 9:2 And His disciples asked Him, saying, Master, who sinned, this man or his parents, that he was born blind?

The leaders of that time even used this mindset to render judgment:

John 9:31 But we know that God does not hear sinners, but if anyone is God-fearing and does His will, He hears him.

In other words, people with a high status viewed people as condemned if they were of a low status, if they were below the line of acceptability, or did not fear God, or did not do His will. Group orientation was so strong and important to the society that they often harmed somebody for benefitting the degraded group; they preferred the word "sacrifice" rather than harm. This was the very logic used by Caiaphas to have Jesus killed. His logic was straightforwardly simple: Better to sacrifice one to save the group.

John 11:48-51 If we let him alone this way, all will believe on him. And the Romans will come and take away both our place and nation. And one of them, Caiaphas, being the high priest of that year, said to them, You do not know anything at all, nor do you consider that it is expedient for us that one man should die for the people, and not that the whole nation perish. And he did not speak this of himself, but being high priest that year, he prophesied that Jesus should die for the nation.

Josephus' narrative about this concept points to the fact that the group is valued more than the individual and that the group comes before the individual.

Our sacrifices are not occasions for drunken self-indulgence - such practices are abhorrent to God - but for sobriety (σωφροσυνην). At these sacrifices prayers for the welfare of the community must take precedence of those for ourselves; for we are born for fellowship (κοινωνια), and he who sets its claims above his private interests is specially acceptable to God. (Against Apion 2. 195-196).

Group orientation minimized individualism and maximized groups. All the power was seated within the group. The group decided *what behavior* was rewarded or punished. The group decided *who* should be rewarded or punished. The group granted such rewards, or executed punishment. The higher the particular group's status the more power it had. Different groups were in competition with each other. They were constantly battling to gain status and to make other groups loose theirs. Group membership was very important. The ultimate punishment was excommunication from a group, forcing a person to join a lower group. The lowest groups, for example, were bands of lepers.

Groups determined status and thereby ruled society through social pressure. Groups enforced conformity. Conformity resulted in stereotypes and compliance. Jesus described the power of this society's love of group rewards as follows:

John 12:43 ... for they loved the glory of men more than the glory of God.

Pierre F. Steenberg, Ph.D., D.Min.

✑ CHAPTER FOUR ✒

TOOL II: HONOR AND SHAME

Unlike most other societies where honor and shame are secondary values, they have been pivotal values to the Mediterranean societies of the New Testament[15]. It was clear that the different groups of people wanted to increase their status and avoid losing status. Then again, how could this be done? What did society use to judge groups to be worthy of higher or lower status, other than sickness and disabilities? What did people do to gain status?

In our western societies people are motivated by money. People would do almost anything to obtain money. If an employer increases a worker's wages, willingness to work harder and longer increases proportionately. The moment the increase is removed, however, the increase in the worker's extra effort and hours also disappears. People's opinions of us are normally less important than earning money.

The New Testament societies did not regard money to be a motivating factor. The only time when money was employed to motivate people had to do with dishonorable behavior:

---

[15] In just about every study on honor and shame the word "pivotal" is used to indicate the prime importance of values during New Testament times. See Hellerman 2000:214.

Mat 28:11-13 And as they were going, behold, some of the guard came into the city and declared all the things that were done to the chief priests.   And being assembled with the elders, and taking counsel, they gave enough silver to the soldiers, saying, Say that His disciples came by night and stole Him away while we slept.

Mat 26:14-15 Then one of the twelve, called Judas Iscariot, went to the chief priests. And he said to them, What will you give me, and I will betray Him to you? And they appointed to him thirty pieces of silver.

The currency of status in the New Testament was honor[16] instead of monetary compensation. Honor had to be limited to have and retain value, just like money[17]. Shortage of honor and the difficulty to obtain it added value to honor. People did everything in their power to gain honor as it was the ultimate prize[18]. Honor was on everyone's mind; so much so that all interaction[19] between people from different groups was an encounter for honor[20]. Honor can be defined as a claim to significance and the social acknowledgment[21] of that worth[22]. Seneca, a first century Roman statesman and philosopher, described honor as follows:

"... that which is honorable is held dear for no other reason than because he is honorable " (De Ben. 4.16.2).

Isocrates, an Athenian orator who was Aristotle's senior, reckoned the value of honor above one's personal safety (Ad Dem. 43). Quintilian, a teacher of rhetoric from the late first century A.D.,

---

[16] Campbell 1995:17-19.
[17] Crook 2006:89.
[18] Hagerdorn and Neyrey 1998:24.
[19] Campbell 2005:26.
[20] Lawrence 2003:144.
[21] Pilch 2002:5.
[22] For a discussion on the definition of honor, see Hellerman 2000:214. Hellerman leans heavily on Malina and Neyrey to construct this definition. Malina and Neyrey's work are cited in the bibliography.

regarded honor as the fundamental factor in persuading people to adopt or avoid a course of action (Institutes 3.8.1).

The various groups determined whether an action resulted in honor or shame[23]. Honor designated a rise in societal esteem while shame indicated a decline. When society judged a person to be honorable that person was granted additional social status. People were treated in accordance with their social status. Conversely, society also dishonored and disgraced people by rejecting them. Honor was prized so highly that it was deemed more valuable than truth or wealth[24]. The love of honor and the fear of shame were so compelling that it caused constant fighting, arguing, belittling, and fear of ostracism[25].

There are many New Testament stories linking people's status with honor. In fact, the highest positions of status were synonymous with the concept "honor":

Mark 15:43 Joseph of Arimathea, an honorable counselor (sic), who also waited for the kingdom of God, came and went in boldly to Pilate and asked for the body of Jesus.

Acts 5:34 Then there stood up one in the Sanhedrin, a Pharisee named Gamaliel, a doctor of the Law honored among all the people. And he commanded the apostles to be put outside a little space.

Acts 13:50 But the Jews stirred up the devout and honorable women, and the chief ones of the city, and raised a persecution against Paul and Barnabas. And they threw them out of their borders.

Acts 17:12 Therefore many of them believed, and quite a few of honorable Greek women and men.

Honor was paramount in everybody's mind; they did everything they could to gain honor, which typically meant conforming to the demands of society. Honor was regarded as such a powerful motivator[26]

---

[23] Campbell 2005:326.
[24] Hellerman 2000:216.
[25] Hagedorn and Neyrey 1998:34.
[26] De Silva 1996.

that people sometimes sought tangible human honor more than the intangible honor that God described. Jesus was the only one to question this practice with the following words:

John 5:44 How can you believe, you who receive honor from one another and do not seek the honor that comes from God only?

People often used worship and religion as means of gaining human honor. Two stories, in particular, come to mind. Honorable people often stood on the street corners to pray. They did so to be seen praying rather than to be communicating with God. Their prayers were fashioned to solicit honor from those who heard them pray. Then, when Jesus taught His disciples not to use vain repetitions in prayer, He was actually informing them that when these people stood on street corners to pray they continuously repeated the same phrases as more people walked by: every time other people walked along the street they would repeat the prayer. In this sense the prayers were actually aimed at passersby rather than God:

Matt 6:5 And when you pray, you shall not be like the hypocrites. For they love to pray standing in the synagogues and in the corners of the streets, so that they may be seen by men. Truly I say to you, they have their reward.

The reward that Jesus spoke of was the honor that people attributed to them because of hearing their prayers. Using worship as a pretense would result in God's condemnation, according to Jesus. Nevertheless, people often exploited religion to bolster their status:

Mark 12:38-40 And He said to them in His teaching, Beware of the scribes, who love to walk about in robes, and love greetings in the markets, and the chief seats in the synagogues, and the uppermost places at feasts who devour widows' houses, and as a pretense make long prayers. These shall receive greater condemnation.

The second set of circumstances where people used worship and religion to gain human honor was with charity: People would donate large sums of money as long as people saw them. Whether their donations were offerings in the synagogue or alms to the poor, it made no difference - as they only donated when people watched. The true reason for giving was not to assist someone in need, but to gain honor. Sometimes offerings to God were also given to be seen and to gain honor.

Jesus also spoke of God attributing honor. Jesus saw honor, rightly used, as rather positive. He used honor as a motivator as it was the currency of status:

John 12:26 If anyone serves Me, let him follow Me; and where I am, there also My servant shall be. If anyone serves Me, the Father will honor him.

There were four basic ways in which people gained honor: Firstly, people were automatically ascribed the same level of honor and status as the family group they were born into[27]. If someone had a king as father, or someone had a father with great honor, they received that amount of honor too. Ben Sira, a scholar and a scribe thoroughly versed in the "Law", confirmed this view when he wrote the following:

"A person's honor comes from his father" (Sir 3:11).

Describing and recounting someone's honor was so important that at someone's death the practice of a eulogy came into being. A eulogy was the practice of celebrating the deceased persons' honor by recounting all honorable deeds of their lives, and also that of their ancestors[28].

Insults were used as a means of challenging people's honor at best, and shaming people at worst[29]. Then again it was not surprising that insults in New Testament times often involved one's ancestors and descendants[30]. Instead of recounting someone's true ancestors people were insulted grievously by being ascribed to the ancestry of someone or something unacceptable[31]:

---

[27] Keener 2005:3.
[28] Plutarch, Moralia 3.
[29] Hellerman 2000:219.
[30] Keener 2005:3.
[31] Simmonds 2009:345.

Matt 3:7 But seeing many of the Pharisees and Sadducees come to his baptism, he said to them, O generation of vipers, who has warned you to flee from the wrath to come?

John 8:44 You are of the Devil as father, and the lusts of your father you will do. He was a murderer from the beginning, and did not abide in the truth because there is no truth in him. When he speaks a lie, he speaks of his own, for he is a liar and the father of it.

Similarly, a person's race became a feature of esteem or lack of honor. In Judea, for example, the classification of being Samaritan not only referred to a certain people, but it was a term of reproach. In order to insult Jesus, for example, they referred to Him as a Samaritan in John 8:48.

Honor could also be gained later in life through adoption[32]. Octavian was adopted by Julius Caesar and, thereby, increasing his honor. In the New Testament Christians are said to be adopted by God and are given the citizenship of heaven. As part of this adoption they are also given the honorable priesthood office:

Phil 3:20-21 For our citizenship is in Heaven, from which also we are looking for the Savior, the Lord Jesus Christ, who shall change our body of humiliation so that it may be fashioned like His glorious body, according to the working of His power, even to subdue all things to Himself.

1 Pet 2:9 But you are a chosen generation, a royal priesthood, a holy nation, a people for possession, so that you might speak of the praises of Him who has called you out of darkness into His marvelous light.

As we saw earlier in Jesus' case He lost honor because of His father and immediate family group.

Secondly, gaining honor was possible through an extraordinary feat. If someone did something significantly people honored that person with an improved status. A soldier, for example, who displays unusual courage, is singled out for special honor. Typically, a king or political

---

[32]   Richards 2008:30.

ruler would ascribe additional honor to the soldier, resulting in more status. There might even be public festivities, inscriptions and declarations to signify higher honor. Since extraordinary feats were exceptional and not typical most people used the third and fourth means of gaining honor:

Thirdly, people gained or lost their honor by means of public debates[33]. In essence, public debates were attempts to gain honor at someone else's expense. This happened by a challenger publically posing a dispute that cannot be answered. The challenged person was now called upon to respond. No response resulted in an automatic defeat and loss of honor. Public bystanders acted as judges to determine who won the debate[34]. Thus, society bestowed honor[35] on the winner and shame on the loser. Honor without public recognition was no honor to begin with. In fact, when someone claimed honor devoid of societal recognition, it led to shame[36]. As a result of both the debate and the public verdict, the winner gained honor from the loser[37].

Consequently, these debates followed a fairly set formula[38]; they took place among equals[39]. The risk for the honorable contestant was just too great if the contest would be lost to an inferior contestant, since one stood to lose a great deal more honor than if the defeat was against an equal. Furthermore, winning a contest against an inferior contestant did not result in much honor since victory is expected – after all, the contestant was inferior.

Thus, these debates could be identified with someone addressing someone else with the same title[40] at which the challenger followed with a question or a challenge[41]. For example, to indicate equal honor a teacher of the law would come to Jesus and say, "...teacher, tell us ..."; or a religious leader would address Jesus as Rabbi, followed by a question:

---

[33] Moxnes 1996:20-21.
[34] Neyrey 1998:26.
[35] Hellerman 2000:218.
[36] Malina and Rohrbaugh 2003:213.
[37] Richards 2008:31.
[38] Campbell 1995:17.
[39] Dixon 1989:41:42.
[40] Esler 2000:333.
[41] Esler 1994:27-29.

Mark 12:14 And coming, they said to Him, Teacher, we know that you are true and you care about no one. For you do not look to the face of men, but teach the way of God in truth. Is it lawful to give tribute to Caesar, or not?

Mark 12:19 Teacher, Moses wrote to us, If a man's brother die and leaves his wife, and leaves no children, his brother should take his wife and raise up seed to his brother.

Matt 21:23-27 And when He had come into the temple, the chief priests and the elders of the people came to Him as He was teaching, and said, By what authority do you do these things? And who gave you this authority? And Jesus answered and said to them, I will also ask you one thing; which if you tell Me, I likewise will tell you by what authority I do these things. The baptism of John, where was it from? From Heaven or from men? And they reasoned within themselves, saying, If we shall say, From Heaven, he will say to us, Why then did you not believe him? But if we shall say From men, we fear the people; for all consider John as a prophet. And they answered Jesus and said, We cannot tell. And He said to them, Neither do I tell you by what authority I do these things.

The religious leaders of the time used this method to attempt to steal away Jesus' honor. If they were successful, Jesus would have been turned into a "lame duck": No one would have listened to Him and no one would have followed Him. This meant that for a great deal Jesus was in competition with them. From the way Jesus responded to these challenges we could see that He was a genius:

Matt 22:46 And no one was able to answer Him a word, nor did anyone dare from that day to question Him anymore.

The result of a challenge or debate was made known by the group granting honor to the winner and treating the loser shamefully. A loss was usually acknowledged by the loser walking away from the scene:

Matt 22:22 When they heard these words, they marveled, and they left Him and went away.

Mark 12:12 And they sought to seize him, but feared the crowd. For they knew that He spoke the parable against them. And leaving Him, they went away.

Lastly, it was possible to gain or lose honor in little increments through daily behavior, for example, being "virtuous" in one's dealings, public prayers, giving to the poor, etc[42]. Aristotle stated that "...the prize appointed for the noblest of deeds...is honor" (Ethics 4.3).

Isocrates advised his students to win both negative and positive challenges to their honor:

"Consider it equally disgraceful to be outdone by your enemies in doing injury and to be surpassed by your friends in doing kindness" (Ad Dem. 26).

The opposite of honor is shame. When a soldier ran away instead of fighting, both he and his family were shamed. When someone was caught in adultery that person was humiliated. When shamed, the entire group's status was lowered. To prevent this from happening, the group often shunned the offender. In certain severe cases the only way the group could regain honor was by the death of the offender. Shame was avoided by avoiding certain behavior deemed to be shameful. When a dishonorable act was committed shame was avoided by concealment and denial[43].

For us to spot the functioning of honor and shame in New Testament society we have to learn the vocabulary associated with honor and shame; examples[44] of these words are as follows:

Glory (δοξα - doxa) (See also glorious, etc.)	*Matt 6:2 Therefore when you do your merciful deeds, do not sound a trumpet before you, as the hypocrites do in the synagogues and in the streets, so that they may have* **glory** *from men. Truly I say to you, They have their reward.*

---

[42] Richards 2008:30.
[43] Hagedorn and Neyrey 1998:36.
[44] Other such example texts are: Rom 13:7; Rom 2:7; Heb 2:9; 2 Pet 1:17; 1 Cor 11:13-15; 2 Cor 9:4.

	*Luke 14:10 But when you are invited, go and recline in the lowest place, so that when he who invited you comes, he may say to you, Friend, go up higher. Then **glory** shall be to you before those reclining with you.*
Honor (τιμη - timē) (See also honorable, etc.)	*John 5:44 How can you believe, you who receive **honor** from one another and do not seek the **honor** that comes from God only?* *Rom 2:10 But He will give glory, **honor** and peace to every man who works good, to the Jew first and also to the Greek.*
Praise (ἐπαινος - epainos)	*Rom 13:3 For the rulers are not a terror to good works, but to the bad. And do you desire to be not afraid of the authority? Do the good, and you shall have **praise** from it.* *1Peter 2:13-14 Then be in obedience to every ordinance of men, because of the Lord, whether to a king as supreme, or to governors as sent by Him for vengeance on evildoers, but for **praise** on well-doers.*
Dishonor (ἀτιμαζω - atimazō)	*John 8:49 Jesus answered, I do not have a demon, but I **honor** My Father, and you dishonor Me.*
Reproach (ὀνειδος - oneidos)	*Luke 1:25 So the Lord has dealt with me in the days in which He looked on me, to take away my **reproach** among men.* *Luke 6:22 Blessed are you when men shall hate you, and when they shall cut you off, and when they shall **reproach** you and shall cast out your name as evil, for the sake of the Son of Man.*
Scorn (καταφρονησις - kataphronēsis)	*Matt 9:24 He said to them, Go back, for the little girl is not dead, but sleeps. And they laughed at Him to **scorn**.*

Slander (λασφημια - blasphēmia)	*Matt 27:39 And those who passed by* **blasphemed** *Him, shaking their heads, ...*

Honor and shame were not only communicated with words, but also in the way the body was treated. The representation of the body could also result in honor or shame: For example, the head of a king was crowned. The head of someone special was anointed. Conversely, however, the face of a prisoner was slapped and their heads were mocked:

Mark 15:17 And they clothed Him with purple and plaited a crown of thorns and put it around His head.

Luke 22:64 And blindfolding Him, they struck Him on His face. And they asked Him, saying, Prophesy! Who is it who struck you?

The physical placement of bodies also represented honor or shame: For example, the king was always seated on a level higher than his subjects. Subjects often bowed low to the ground to acknowledge the king's higher status and honor. After a war, enemies were often paraded naked as a form of shaming. In addition, they were also thrown at the feet of their victors:

1 Cor 15:24-25 then is the end, when He delivers the kingdom to God, even the Father; when He makes to cease all rule and all authority and power. For it is right for Him to reign until He has put all the enemies under His feet.

Remember that people believed that the sick were sick because they were sinners; and sinners had no honor. Thus, they were treated disrespectfully. Their bodies were placed low down to denote their shame:

Matt 15:30 And great crowds came to Him, having with them the lame, blind, dumb, maimed, and many others. And they cast them down at Jesus' feet...

One day as Jesus was walking along a great crowd followed him. In the multitude people bumped and pushed against Jesus, as usually happened in a crowd. A woman touched Jesus to be healed; He stopped and inquired about her touching Him. At this point the woman was embarrassed; she was considered to be a sinner because of her illness. To demonstrate her lowly place in society she lowered the position of her body when she talked to Jesus:

Mark 5:33 But the woman, fearing and trembling, knowing what had been done in her, came and fell down before Him and told Him all the truth.

People wished to avoid shame at all cost. Joseph, Jesus' earthly dad, wished to avoid shame when he found out that Mary was pregnant prior to their marriage. To escape the shame, which such pregnancies caused, he wanted to leave her. Simply, most men would have walked away; after all, the pregnancy was not his doing. They wished to minimize the shame brought on to them for being closely associated with immoral people. Then, as Joseph loved Mary deeply he wished to do his best to minimize her shame. The point of Joseph's intended action unmistakably was to hide her shame from this group-oriented society:

Matt 1:19 But Joseph, her husband to be, being just, and not willing to make her a public example, he purposed to put her away secretly.

Honor brought great reward in this society, but shame came at an equally great price. These values shaped society, behavior and thinking. These values were the driving force behind what people did, how they did it, and what was made public, or was hidden from the public.

In conclusion then, people sought after the approval of others and did their best to avoid disapproval. People's behavior was shaped by the group's definition of what was honorable. People refrained from behavior which brought reproach and caused the person's estimation to drop in the eyes of others. The desire to be honored was of great value, which ensured the members' cooperation to promote the health and survival of the group. In return, the group would reward honorable behavior by bestowing honor to the person involved. The group also employed measures to disgrace and shame transgressors. Honor and shame was used to coerce conformity[45] to society[46].

---

[45] Richards 2008:34.
[46] Steenberg 2000:149.

Pierre F. Steenberg, Ph.D., D.Min.

CHAPTER FIVE

TOOL III: FOUR DISTINCT GROUPS

It is so easy to make the mistake of thinking that all the New Testament people belonged to one large group called the Jews. This thinking may be compared with thinking that all Christians believe the same doctrine and have the same convictions today, or that all Christians worship in the same way. Obviously, Christians do not all believe the same dogmas and doctrines nor do they all praise and worship in the same way. Some Christians believe in the "secret rapture", for example, while others believe in the "second coming"; some believe in the immortality of the soul, others believe in purgatory, the place where "souls" remain until they have expiated their sins and can go to heaven, while still others believe that the dead are dead until the coming of the Lord. During worship some churches consider it reverent to be quiet, yet quietness is viewed as being spiritually "dead" by others. There is no such thing as a Christian "group" to which all Christians belong, believing the same and worshipping in the same way. Similarly, the Jews of the New Testament were also partitioned into different groups. These groups believed different doctrines, had a different emphasis on certain beliefs and sometimes even fought against each other.

There were many Jewish subgroups in New Testament times, but only four groups deserve attention here. They were the Pharisees, Sadducees, Essenes, and a fourth group, which included the Zealots. The following story is presented to demonstrate how these groups differed, fought against one another and how Paul used the divisions between these groups to his advantage. Also take note of the struggle for honor and avoidance of shame between the two sides by striking Paul "on the mouth" and Paul calling them "a whitened wall".

> *Acts 23:2-7 And the high priest Ananias commanded those who stood by him to strike him on the mouth. Then Paul said to him, God shall strike you, whitened wall! For do you sit judging me according to the Law, and against the law command me to be stricken? And they who stood by him said, Do you revile God's high priest? Then Paul said, I did not know, brothers, that he was the high priest; for it is written, "You shall not speak evil of the ruler of your people." But when Paul saw that the one part were **Sadducees** and the other part **Pharisees**, he cried out in the Sanhedrin, Men! Brothers! I am a Pharisee, the son of a Pharisee! I am being judged because of the hope and resurrection of the dead. And when he had said this, there arose a dissension between the Pharisees and the Sadducees; and the multitude was divided.* (Emphasis added).

Paul has been accused before this group of Jews, but it is interesting to note that there are two subgroups present here – Pharisees and Sadducees. Of much interest is the fact that the high priest probably belonged to the Sadducees[47].

> *Acts 5:17 And rising up, the high priest, and all those who were with him (which is the sect of the Sadducees) were filled with anger...*

As has been mentioned before, slapping someone in the face or on the mouth was not always meant to induce pain; the purpose was rather to put the person to shame. It was one of the ways in which those with honor degraded the honor of the one that was being slapped. Ananias' command to strike Paul was intended for the degrading of his honor.

---

[47] It is important to note that the high priests were connected to the Sadducees (Kanter 2004:6), but it is equally important to note that the Sadducees did not share the same scope and authority as the high priests (cf. Oakman 1997:788). We know that Caiaphas was in fact a Sadducee (Regev 2006:126).

Paul's response to this challenge of his honor was to shame the high priest, first of all by calling him "a whitened wall": Beautiful on the outside but "corrupt on the inside"!

Secondly, Paul shamed Ananias by using a counter accusation by which Paul substantiates the *name,* "whitened wall". Ananias is judging according to the law - good and well — "the whiteness of the wall", but then, according to Paul, he gives a command which goes against the law, "corrupt on the inside".

Thirdly, Ananias is shamed by Paul, denying the high priest the honor typically associated with his position ("I did not know, brothers, that he was the high priest"). The battle for honor was very clear here.

Now the battle got interesting as Paul noticed that some were Pharisees and others Sadducees. Paul also knew that the Sadducees did not believe in life after death or in the resurrection as the Pharisees believed.

Act 23:8 For the Sadducees say that there is no resurrection, neither angel, nor spirit; but the Pharisees confess both.

Thus far there were these two subgroups that formed one bigger group against Paul. Paul had no chance to offer a defense and win. So, he united with one group, "Brothers! I am a Pharisee". He deliberately used the salutation, "brothers", to achieve this. By stating that he was the son of a Pharisee he is also claiming the same extent of honor as they have due to birth[48]. Thus, Paul just divided the larger group again into two smaller subgroups.

The next step was to use the doctrinal differences and animosity between these groups to his advantage: He stated that he was being accused of "the hope and resurrection of the dead". The Pharisees could not accuse Paul of this belief because they also believed it. The Sadducees, however, thought that this doctrine was heretical. The result was exactly as planned — the two groups fought with each other rather than with Paul.

This was not an isolated incident of these two groups being at odds with one another, or being divided into two different groups.

---

[48] Richards 2008:30.

Matt 22:34 But hearing that He had silenced the Sadducees, the Pharisees were gathered together.

The Pharisees

A great deal of what is known of the Pharisees is found in the writings of Josephus. The Pharisees were already a discrete group by approximately 100 B.C. Josephus describes the Pharisees as:

"...a party of Jews which seems to be more religious than the others and to explain the laws with more minute care" (War I:110).

Josephus also made it known that the Pharisees were sophisticated and friendly to strangers (War 2:166). They were very popular and were followed by the masses (Antiq.13:298)[49]. They came mostly from the middle classes[50]. Moreover, not all the people belonging to a specific group had the same convictions; even within the Pharisaic group there were compelling divisions. At the end of the first century B.C., for example, two famous Rabbis, Shammai and Hillel, led two different schools of thought and had two differing interpretations of the law. Just for the record, Shammai was more conservative and Hillel was more liberal.

The main point to remember about the Pharisees is that their purpose was to interpret and define the law[51]. Whenever they had a problem with Jesus it was about the law. Whenever they had a debate in a tussle with Jesus to shame Him, they chose a topic which they knew best – the law.

Matt 22:35-36 Then one of them, a lawyer, asked, tempting Him and saying, Master, which is the great commandment in the Law?

---

[49] Friedrichsen 2005:106.

[50] It is disputed whether or not there was a middle class. There is much evidence of the Pharisees being subservient bureaucrats (Friedrichsen 2005:107). "Subservient" certainly does not point to the highest class, yet the word "bureaucrat" also does not suggest they were from a lower class. Although a type of middle class may have been very small, it is hard to imagine how else to interpret their position (Saldarini 1988).

[51] Oakman 199:788.

Matt 12:2 But when the Pharisees saw, they said to Him, Behold, your disciples do that which it is not lawful to do on the Sabbath day.

Matt 15:1-2 Then the scribes and Pharisees who were from Jerusalem came to Jesus, saying, why do your disciples transgress the tradition of the elders? For they do not wash their hands when they eat bread.

Mark 7:3 For the Pharisees and all the Jews do not eat unless they immerse their hands with the fist, holding the tradition of the elders.

Matt 19:3 And the Pharisees came to Him, tempting Him and saying to Him, Is it lawful for a man to put away his wife for every cause?

Because of their obsession with the law Pharisees were often called "lawyers". This term is not to be confused by the legal concept, "lawyer". A lawyer in New Testament stories refers to someone who is educated in the Old Testament law and Pharisees were knowledgeable in the law. They were not lawyers in Roman law, defending people in court. Perhaps, Jesus summarized them in the best way when He said the following:

Matt 23:2-3 The scribes and the Pharisees sit in Moses' seat. Therefore whatever they tell you to observe, observe and do. But do not do according to their works; for they say, and do not do.

"Sitting in Moses' seat" here meant that they were little imitations of Moses, and that they were taking Moses' place by "giving" or providing the law. Many Pharisaic formulations or interpretations of the law are actually found in the New Testament. One example will suffice:

Matt 23:16 Woe to you, blind guides, saying, Whoever shall swear by the temple, it is nothing; but whoever shall swear by the gold of the temple, he is a debtor.

The Pharisees never intended sayings, for example, this one, to be thought of lightly; rather, this saying was intended to prevent people from being held accountable for "casual" oaths. When Moses' law commands people to honor their fathers and mothers Pharisees thought that they should assist people to keep this law by defining which behavior was honorable and which conduct was not. When Moses' law commanded people to keep the Sabbath day holy Pharisees thought that it would be helpful to know what "keeping the Sabbath holy" meant and what exactly would constitute the transgressing of the Sabbath law. Consequently, they formulated many laws, defining anew previously existing laws. Here is an example of a pharisaical law, which defined an existing law further:

> *Acts 1:12 Then they returned to Jerusalem from the mount Of Olive Grove, which is a Sabbath day's journey from Jerusalem.*

Just in case you were wondering how far a "Sabbath day's journey" was, the actual distance was continuously being changed every time the religious leaders reinterpreted the law. By the time we got into the New Testament periods, however, Pharisees thought this distance was just over a mile from your home, and of course people were allowed to walk back home, making it effectively just over two miles. Thus, Pharisees were primarily concerned with the law, and its interpretation; the law's interpretation is often called "the tradition of the elders".

Jesus assumed the role of "teacher of the law". Jesus was rapidly becoming the religious leader, whilst the Pharisees thought they were the religious leaders. Jesus drew great crowds regularly, often thousands of people. People came to Jesus with questions of scriptural interpretation. Jesus was not only stepping on their turf, but also on their toes. He was taking their place.

> *Matt 9:35-36 And Jesus went about all the cities and villages, teaching in their synagogues, and preaching the gospel of the kingdom, and healing every sickness and every disease among the people. But seeing the crowds, He was moved with compassion on them, because they were tired and scattered like sheep having no shepherd.*

According to the Pharisees, who viewed themselves as the religious shepherds of the people, and as the teachers of the law and the moral compass of society[52], Jesus was "stealing" the people from them. Just imagine the insult to them when a lawyer asked *Jesus* to interpret the law. Such a lawyer must have been seen as a traitor of any Pharisee.

The Sadducees

Josephus told us that the group of Sadducees was largely made up of rich aristocrats. They did not accept the interpretations of the Pharisees and only believed what was written in the Pentateuch, the first five books of the Hebrew Scriptures. Neither did they share the belief in the resurrection, in angels or spirits[53].

> *Acts 23:8 For the Sadducees say that there is no resurrection, neither angel, nor spirit; but the Pharisees confess both.*

> *Matt 22:23 On that day the Sadducees came to Him, who say that there is no resurrection. And they asked Him.*

Since angels were mentioned in the Old Testament and since there were also prophecies related to the resurrection in the Old Testament, and since the Sadducees did not believe in angels or the resurrection one would come to the conclusion that Sadducees did not accept the rest of the Old Testament outside the Pentateuch. Perhaps this was what Jesus was referring to when He said to them:

> *Matt 22:29 Jesus answered and said to them, You err, not knowing the Scriptures nor the power of God.*

The primary concern of the Sadducees during the New Testament times was sacrifices. Since sacrifices took place in the temple, the temple was their domain. They seemed either to be priests, or at the very least, they were very closely aligned with the priests[54]. The centrality of the priesthood was one of their primary concerns[55].

---

[52] Moessner 1988:30.
[53] For more differences between Pharisees and Sadducees see the study of Regev 2005.
[54] Regev 2005:188.
[55] Regev 2006:135.

Sacrifices were the very essence of the survival of the priests; it was their livelihood[56]. Perhaps this is the reason why they were so much against any talk of a resurrection. The resurrection would mean an end to sacrifices and consequently, an end to them, constituted as a group – the end of life as they knew it. They had everything to lose and, therefore, were very involved in solving the "Jesus problem". The high priest played a key role in the trials of Jesus. As demonstrated earlier on, the high priest was also a Sadducee[57]. When Jesus spoke of breaking down the temple in three days, the Sadducees were more distressed than the other groups.

A secondary concern of Sadducees was doctrine. Sadducees were more doctrinally conservative than the rabbis[58]. They also stressed priestly prominence over against ordinary people[59]. As seen above, Matthew 22:23 demonstrated how the Sadducees had doctrinal issues against Jesus. They also had doctrinal issues against Peter. In fact, it seemed as if doctrine was the very reason why they seized Peter and John:

> *Acts 4:1-2 And as they spoke to the people, the priests, and the temple commander, and the Sadducees came on them, being grieved that they taught the people, even to announce through Jesus the resurrection from the dead.*

The Essenes

The Essenes, who lived around Qumran, were not really mentioned in the New Testament. Yet much is known about them through the writings of contemporary historians, and since the discovery of the Qumran scrolls much more has been learned about them[60]. These

---

[56] There are recorded debates between the Sadducees and the Pharisees about whether or not people should pay to sacrifice in the temple. Needless to say, the Sadducees wanted the people to pay while the Pharisees wanted the general population to subsidize sacrifices. It is clear from information such as this that the Sadducees' livelihood was tied up in the temple. Evidence also suggested that the Sadducees managed the temple taxes: see Haskell 2008:176.

[57] Kanter 2004:6.

[58] Regev 2006:128.

[59] Regev 2006:128, 135.

[60] Goranson 1990:70.

people did not only live in Qumran as there is evidence of an Essene community in Jerusalem. One had to go through a long process to become an Essene. Josephus viewed the Essenes as being just as important as the Pharisees and Sadducees.

The primary concern of the Essenes was purity. That is why they lived a secluded, isolated, and an exclusive life[61]. They withdrew themselves for fear of losing their purity. They did not wish to be polluted by the evils of others. Consequently, they did not interact a great deal with Jesus, yet it is important to note that they would have had a huge influence on the New Testament Jews rejecting Jesus and withdrawing from Him, if they viewed Jesus as being impure.

The Zealots

The only concern of this group was "the holy land". They had to do all they could to secure the land. After all, "God gave the land to them". It was considered their duty to get the foreigners out of *their* land. This included the Romans, Samaritans and any other group inhabiting their land. The Zealots were often known to have used violence and led revolts to achieve this purpose.

It was probably due to this group that tax collectors were deemed sinners with no honor. Tax collecting on behalf of the Romans was seen as treason. They would not have taken too kindly to Jesus' reply to a tax question that people should "give unto Caesar what is Caesar's". This group took their task so seriously that their very name fashioned the English word "zeal". Their name became synonymous with "giving yourself completely".

Gal 1:14 And I progressed in Judaism beyond many contemporaries in my race, being much more a zealot of the traditions of my fathers.

1 Cor 14:12 Even so you, since you are zealots of spiritual things, seek to build up the church, in order that you may abound.

---

[61] Goranson 1990:70.

The Impact of these Four Groups on Jesus

Many people think that Jesus was rejected because the New Testament Jews expected the Messiah to overthrow the Roman yoke and reestablish the Jewish kingdom. This, however, is only true of the Zealots and their influence on others. Zealots were looking for a Messiah who was going to reestablish an earthly kingdom. Once again the land would be their land. No foreigners would inhabit the land. They would regain their sovereignty. As we saw, however, Jesus did not appear as a likely candidate to accomplish this purpose, therefore, they did not really interact a great deal with Jesus as they realized that He did not share their agenda.

Similarly, the other groups did not accept Jesus as the Messiah because He was not what they were looking for in a Messiah. They were looking for different qualities in the Messiah which were not necessarily limited to overthrowing the Romans. In fact, overthrowing the Roman yoke was not as important to the other groups. Make no mistake, all New Testament Jews would have loved their own sovereignty, but their Messiah had to comply with other conditions too.

The Pharisees rejected Jesus because, according to them, He was a lawbreaker as Jesus supposedly "harvested" grain on the Sabbath, healed on the Sabbath, and even instructed a person to carry his bed on the Sabbath; and a lawbreaker could never be the promised Messiah. Moreover, Jesus rejected their interpretation of the law: Instead, Jesus presented His own interpretation, which contradicted theirs. This "breaking of the law" and contradicting interpretations turned out to be a non-negotiable "deal breaker" to a group to whom the law was everything.

The Sadducees rejected Jesus because, according to them, He was doctrinally deficient and, most of all Jesus supposedly opposed the sacrificial system. Jesus even threatened to "break down the temple". "No temple" would mean no sacrifices and no sacrifices would mean no priests. When John declared Jesus the "Passover Lamb" he stated that Jesus was the fulfillment of sacrifice. In fact, the teaching of Jesus being the sacrifice meant that they had to make a choice between accepting Jesus, which would result in the termination of their existence by way of income, lifestyle, status, need to society, etc., and by rejecting Jesus would result in the salvation of everything they considered important parts of their existence. They could not fathom that the Messiah would bring an end to everything dear to them. Nowhere was this choice more evident than in the cleansing of the temple, which happened twice - Matthew, Mark, and Luke clearly had Jesus cleansing the temple during the final week prior to the crucifixion [Matt 21:12-13; Mark 11:15-17; Luke 19:45-46]. John tells us that Jesus cleansed the temple between turning the water into wine [John 2:1-12] and His encounter with Nicodemus [John 3:1-21] at the beginning of His ministry – thus, there were two cleanings)[62].

Jesus threatened the very existence and livelihood of the Sadducees. Surely, they must have thought that God would never do such a thing. After all, it was God who instituted sacrifice and a true Messiah would not go against God.

The Essenes would have rejected Jesus because He mixed and mingled with sinners, prostitutes, well, people who were considered to be impure. They would not have rejected Jesus only because such associations were detrimental to their honor, but, because the Messiah would not be impure, or would mix with those who were not pure. After all, a rotten apple spoils the box. The true Messiah had to be an example, and a leader who would show them the way of purity. Jesus' way was incongruent with their understanding of God's way of purity; therefore, Jesus could not have been from God. Jesus should have withdrawn from such lowly people.

Not only did Jesus' actions go against the philosophy of the Essenes, but also His teachings. According to the Essenes Jesus' teaching of being the "salt of the earth" made no sense:

Matt 5:13 You are the salt of the earth, but if the salt loses its savor, with what shall it be salted? It is no longer good for anything, but to be thrown out and to be trodden underfoot by men.

The Essenes would have loved the part that they should not "lose their savor", but they believed that savor is preserved by withdrawing. They believed it to be impossible to be the salt of the

---

[62] There is quite a debate as to whether or not two temple clearings are academically defensible. As usual, the whole gamut of opinions is available. For an academic discussion on this topic see Richards 2008.

earth and yet to keep one's savor. Replying to a question from the scribes and Pharisees why Jesus mingled with sinners His answer was directly the opposite from what the Essenes wanted to hear. First of all, Jesus placed Himself in a position conducive to pollution. Good Essenes would never have placed them in such a position to begin with. Secondly, Jesus' answer is not some excuse as to why it accidentally or unavoidably happened; instead He stated that it was very deliberate.

Luke 5:31 And Jesus answered and said to them, Those who are sound do not need a physician, but those who are sick.

With this outlook on life and its purpose where Jesus was reaching out, and the Essenes lived exclusively for purity's sake, their different convictions were very much incompatible and directly opposed to each other. Thus, by and large, the Essenes withdrew from Jesus.

All four groups had "problems" with Jesus. All four groups rejected Jesus, but for very different reasons. Yet, the biggest challenge and threat to Jesus came from the Pharisees and Sadducees. As long as the Essenes were in their shells they were safe from the influence of Jesus and had nothing to lose from Him. The Zealots had enough experience dealing with people like Jesus who were not bothered by Rome. They were used to seeing the Jewish rulers making deals with the Romans. They watched Jewish people "side" with Rome by collecting taxes. Jesus was seen just as one more on the "other side". They were not threatened by Jesus; they would just accomplish their goals according to their way.

The Pharisees and Sadducees on the other hand stood to lose everything. The Pharisees were losing the people and their role as leaders and interpreters of the law to Jesus[63]. The Sadducees were losing proper doctrine to the "heresy" of Jesus, in addition to their priestly roles and sacrifices. Hence, the whole time these two groups were at odds with Jesus. Strangely enough, it was the very people, whom the Pharisees and Sadducees were losing to Jesus, who protected Jesus from the Pharisees and Sadducees, without even knowing it. In any event, the tension of people siding with Jesus rather than with the Pharisees was especially evident:

---

[63] Driggers 2007, 235.

Matt 21:46 But seeking to lay hands on Him, they feared the crowd, because they held Him for a prophet.

❧ CHAPTER SIX ❧

TOOL IV: DIFFERENT WORLD VIEWS

Every person has a way of looking at and making sense of the world, for example, some believe themselves to be victims and they look to society and the government to "save" and "support" them. Because of their "victim status" they are convinced that they are entitled to be assisted, to be restored and that they are "privileged" to be assisted. They are convinced that society owes them, as they feel victimized.

On the other hand, some believe that people have to contribute to society to make it work. This group looks at the "victims" as a drain on society for they do not contribute to society, but rather demand sustenance. Yet, the "victims" view the "contributors" as the perpetrators – it is this group's fault that they are victimized in the first place.

We are not going to give a ruling which side is right, and that is not the purpose of presenting the topic. The argument is that all people without exception perceive, think, and believe according to different world views or paradigms. These world views actually assist us to make sense of our world. We use these views to interpret what happens. Views of different people or groups of people are often in conflict with others.

The New Testament people were no different, for they too subscribed to different world views. These views of life influenced their interpretation of events and they used them to attempt to influence other groups. For our purposes here it will suffice to look at the New Testament world views comprehending four components which make up most societies. These constituents are the following:

Politics
Economics
Religion/Ideology
Kinship/Family Life[64].

The discussion in this chapter will be limited to the world views of the Jews and the Romans. We acknowledge that there has been no global Jewish view to which all Jews have subscribed, just as we have discussed the four different Jewish groups in a previous chapter. Every person thought differently and relied on different world view paradigms. For the purpose of this discussion we will remain vague and talk about generalities to which most Jews and Romans, living in the New Testament period, would agree. It is valuable to work with vagueness and imprecision, as more people agree on broad principles rather than on subtle and refined ideas. Before these four topics as world views are discussed, let us briefly look at what we mean when by politics, economics, religion/ideology and kinship.

Politics

This discussion would be limited to politics as it relates to governmental reigning, ruling, decision-making and enforcement. In essence the New Testament concept of politics was equated to power[65]. In past history nations were self-governing, while at other times, such as in the New Testament, one nation, for example, the Romans, ruled another nation, the Jews. During times of transition between self-rule and oppressive rule we often find war. Politics is about power; power is gained militarily, economically, or by other means. The political interpretation of the "golden rule", "… whatever you desire that men should do to you, do even so to them …" (Matt 7:12), is, *"The one with the gold rules".*

---

[64] May 1997:207.
[65] May 1997:2009.

Economics

For our purpose here the concept economics will be limited to wealth, as money is just one form of wealth and prosperity, or the lack thereof. Drought, wars, taxation, politics and many other factors influenced the economy.

Religion/Ideology

Faith and ideological convictions relate to people's life journeys. Questions about religion include: Where do we come from? Where are we going? What is our purpose in life? Morality also fits into this component. Basically religion has to do with how people deal with other people, and how God and a person deals with each other. An ideology is a body of ideas, aspiring to be a total supreme system in control of our thoughts and lives.

Kinship/family

Family has always been important. In fact, Rome considered the family as a major building block of society. The question remains, however, exactly who is part of the family and who not? What are the privileges and responsibilities of the family towards family members, and towards people who are not family? Kinship has to do with the interaction of this complex unit, called family.

These different components all interact with one another and sometimes they overlap. "Politics" exists within the family. The "economy" can drive "politics", and *vice versa*. The "economy" affects the "family", and "family" dynamics influence the "economy". All four components are actually intertwined with each other. The question is: which of these components are the most important? Otherwise, we can ask the same question from a different perspective: Which components have the most influence over the others, and if forced to choose between conflicting values of these components, what will be chosen, and why? Is there any particular element which overrides and influences the other three more? Perhaps one component shapes and determines all the others more; consequently, the others are seen in the light of this overriding influence. In general, societies were fragmented, just as today.

This fragmentation also applied to the New Testament societies. This fragmentation, however, has to be limited, to leave a few core values for a group, society, or nation intact, to be able to regard it still a group, a society, or a nation. There have to be some elements in common to bond and keep them together as a group otherwise they would not be functioning as units. In reconstructing New Testament societies those core elements need to be identified and understood. At the basic level the New Testament Jews agreed as a group or nation on the following world views concerning these four components, which form a nation.

The Generalized New Testament Jewish World View

Religion was seen at the center of the other three components, politics, economics and kinship/family. New Testament Jews regarded religion as the overarching component through which the other three world views were seen. Often political arguments were composed by means of religion, demonstrating its priority[66]. In fact, it was believed that religion was the reason behind the other three sections, playing out the way they did. For example, they believed it was because of their unfaithfulness to God, which is their religious view, that they were politically ruled by others. New Testament Jews believed that God was in charge of political life.

> *Luke 1:68-75 Blessed is the Lord, the God of Israel, for He has visited and redeemed His people and has raised up a horn of salvation for us in the house of His servant David, as He spoke by the mouth of His holy prophets from eternity; that we should be saved from our enemies and from the hand of all who hate us, to perform the mercy promised to our fathers, and to remember His holy covenant, the oath which He swore to our father Abraham, that He would grant to us, that we, being delivered out of the hand of our enemies, might serve Him without fear in holiness and righteousness before Him all the days of our life.*

It was God who redeemed His people politically and saved them from their enemies. Once delivered from their enemies, they may once

---

[66] Driggers 2007:235.

again serve God without fear, which again is their religious view. Consequently, religion defined how they viewed and interpreted politics. It was God who established political powers and provided political authority to accomplish religious purposes.

> *Luke 1:32 He shall be great and shall be called the Son of the Highest. And the Lord God shall give Him the throne of His father David.*

> *Matt 9:8 But when the crowds saw, they marveled and glorified God, who had given such authority to men.*

> *Matt 28:18 And Jesus came and spoke to them, saying, All authority is given to Me in Heaven and in earth.*

> *John 5:26-27 For as the Father has life in Himself, so He has given to the Son to have life within Himself, and has given Him authority to execute judgment also, because He is the Son of Man.*

> *John 10:18 No one takes it (my life) from Me, but I lay it down from Myself. I have authority to lay it down, and I have authority to take it again. I have received this commandment from My Father.*

It may be argued that Jesus' authority was viewed differently because He stated that God had sent Him. At the time of their writing after the time of Jesus His disciples knew who He was and thus, may have viewed His authority in a different light than other "earthly" rulers; however, this was *not* the case. It was believed that even so-called earthly rulers received their authority from God; this included pagan rulers. All authority came from God as religion was the overarching component, controlling politics. This can be seen in the way Paul argues about politics as a topic, for example, his whole motivation for political adherence and obedience was religiously motivated:

> *Rom 13:1-2 Let every soul be subject to the higher authorities. For there is no authority but of God; the authorities that exist are ordained by God. So that the one resisting the authority resists the*

ordinance of God; and the ones who resist will receive judgment to themselves.

Religion was a great deal more important than politics. If religion and politics would clash and believers were faced with a choice between them, they mostly chose religion. The New Testament view that religion was the overarching value was clear – religion came before politics. In the case of Acts 5:29 Peter faced the choice of adhering to the Sanhedrin's political authority, even though the topic was religious; it was a question of political authority versus obedience to God:

Acts 5:29 And Peter and the apostles answered and said, We ought to obey God rather than men.

Similarly, if the economy became bearish, and there were unfavorable economic conditions, they considered it to be God's way of influencing life. If a family suffers, it must be because of its sins, because of its religion, or lack of correct religion. Jesus Himself taught that it was God who provided what we need. Jesus even tied God's providence to a person's relationship with God:

Matt 6:25-26 Therefore I say to you, Do not be anxious for your life, what you shall eat, or what you shall drink; nor for your body, what you shall put on. Is not life more than food, and the body more than clothing? Behold the birds of the air; for they sow not, nor do they reap, nor gather into barns. Yet your heavenly Father feeds them; are you not much better than they are?

Matt 6:30-33 Therefore if God so clothes the grass of the field, which today is, and tomorrow is thrown into the oven, will He not much rather clothe you, little-faiths? Therefore do not be anxious, saying, what shall we eat? or, What shall we drink? or, With what shall we be clothed? For the nations seek after all these things. For your heavenly Father knows that you have need of all these things. But seek first the kingdom of God and His righteousness; and all these things shall be added to you.

Armed with many Old Testament stories, they believed that God provided rain, and He caused drought. God's decision to cause rain or drought was related to their religion. Consequently, religion determined economic wellbeing or hardship.

> *James 5:17-18 Elijah was a man of like passion as we are. And he prayed earnestly that it might not rain, and it did not rain on the earth for the time of three years and six months. And he prayed again, and the heaven gave rain, and the earth caused its fruit to sprout.*

There is enough evidence to show that this Old Testament view was also viable during the New Testament period. The obvious point is that religion is the overarching component over the economy.

> *Matt 5:45 so that you may become sons of your Father in Heaven. For He makes His sun to rise on the evil and on the good, and sends rain on the just and on the unjust.*

> *Acts 14:17 And yet He did not leave Himself without witness, doing good, giving rain and fruitful season to us from heaven, filling our hearts with food and gladness.*

Kinship too was governed and considered through the religious lens. Religion served as the motivator of relationships. All the roles of husbands, wives, slaves and family were defined by religion. Religion determined how these roles were perceived.

> *1Tim 5:8 But if anyone does not provide for his own, and especially his family, he has denied the faith and is worse than an infidel.*

> *Col 3:18-23 Wives, be subject to your own husbands, as is becoming in the Lord. Husbands, love your wives, and do not be bitter against them. Children, obey your parents in all things, for this is well-pleasing to the Lord. Fathers, do not provoke your children, lest they be discouraged. Slaves, obey your masters according to the flesh in all things; not with eye-service, as men-pleasers, but in singleness of heart, fearing God. And whatever you do, do it heartily, as to the Lord and not to men.*

Eph 5:23-25 For the husband is the head of the wife, even as Christ is the head of the church; and He is the Savior of the body. Therefore as the church is subject to Christ, so let the wives be to their own husbands in everything. Husbands, love your wives, even as Christ also loved the church and gave Himself for it.

Religion was also seen to be behind the ability or inability to conceive or give birth. Kinship was unmistakably shaped, motivated and observed through the overarching component of religion. Religion, then, was the lens through which every aspect of life was observed. Kinship, politics and economics were almost regarded as sub-categories of religion. Religion shaped not only their interpretation of the other three world views, but they believed that religion actually shaped the other three world views directly. When their religion went well, the other three areas went well too. When they failed religiously, the other three world views fell apart. Religion also provided reasons for their behaviour regarding each of the other segments of society, politics, economics and kinship. The other three areas did not really influence their religious views; it was always the other way around. Religion, then, dominated, and dictated to, the other three world views. Graphically the four world views according the New Testament Jews would look like the following display:

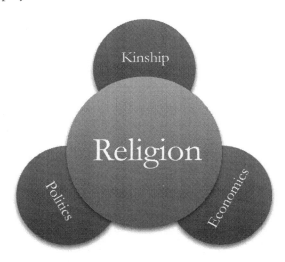

The New Testament Jewish World View

Unlike the New Testament Jews the Romans did not view religion as their main component of society, shaping the other components. Romans would not ask how religion could shape the other elements of society when there were such a variety of religions, so many gods and such a diversity of religious views. Jews did not have to deal with this problem as they did not have any other religion or belief in other gods – they were monotheists. The Roman thought pattern contained a world view comprising a variety of religions and numerous gods - polytheism. They had no problem adding additional gods as they learned about other religions along the way. Religion was one of the sub-categories of the Romans; their main component was politics. For them politics was at the center of everything. The Romans used religion to build and advance their political empire. Other religions were accepted and incorporated into their religion, as long as these religions upheld and supported the Roman Empire.

The family, that is kinship, was simply seen as the building block of the political empire. Families would provide the stability for the political system; they were regarded for providing the workforce behind the generation of taxes. Families provided units and components for law and order, rather than being unconnected chaotic parts of the system. All family affairs were regarded by the Romans either as strength and political gain, or weakness and political loss.

Political power over others resulted in the collection of taxes, which were the main source of revenue for the Romans. So, the economic state of affairs was related to political rule. If the political control was lost, taxes would be lost; therefore, political reign was of the utmost importance.

Many nations deified their kings during the Old Testament times. The Romans also observed their highest political ruler as a type of god; thus, homage, reverence, worship and religious honor were also shaped by politics. Refusal to partake in Roman "religious" feasts, for example, was seen as political protest and punished politically. Politics was the lens through which all facets of society were viewed.

Matt 27:15 Now at that feast the governor was accustomed to release to the people a prisoner, whomever they desired.

The feast, mentioned above in the text, was the Jewish Passover. Even though the Romans did not celebrate the Passover, the Jewish religious feasts were used by the Romans for political gain. The Jews often brought people to the Romans for judgment because of religious reasons; however, the Romans' decisions were often based on political gain rather than considering the religious merits of cases.

> *Acts 12:1-3 And at that time Herod the king threw on his hands to oppress some of those of the church. … And because he saw it pleased the Jews, he went further to seize Peter also. (And they were days of Unleavened Bread.)*

> *Acts 24:27 But after two years Felix welcomed a successor, Porcius Festus. And wishing to show a favor to the Jews, Felix left Paul bound.*

> *Acts 25:9 But Festus, wanting to please the Jews, answered Paul and said, Will you go up to Jerusalem and be judged there before me about these things?*

The Jews had religious problems with Paul. The Romans did not care much about these types of problems, but used the religious issues politically to gain Jewish favor. Thus, we can see how the Jews situated religion in the center of societal components, while the Romans assigned politics to the center. It is important to notice the difference between the Jewish graphical representation of these four world views and that of the Romans:

The New Testament Roman World View

The Jews understood that the Roman world view was politically centered. They also realized that Rome's view of religion was a great deal different from their own. This meant that they knew they could not use pure and merely religious reasons for getting someone convicted by the Romans. Often the Jews had religious problems, but they could get their way only if they presented them to the Romans as political problems. It is rather interesting to watch the interaction between Jewish religion and Roman politics.

The Jews could not succeed by using religious charges against Paul, as he was not a political threat to the Romans. Paul did not violate any Roman civil or political laws. In fact, Roman confusion characterizes Paul's trials, just compare Acts 21–26. It is significant to listen how the Romans speak of the Jew's accusations:

Acts 23:29 whom I found be accused of questions of their law, and having no charge worthy of death or of bonds.

The accusations were on some "questions of *their* law". The Romans attempted to regard the Jewish religious charges as legal or political issues rather than as religious affairs. Furthermore, Paul was not found guilty of a "charge worthy of death", because the charges concerned *their* religious laws rather than the Roman political or civil laws. There are many examples of this:

Acts 25:25 But I had perceived nothing he had committed worthy of death, and that he himself has appealed to Augustus, I determined to send him…

Acts 26:31 And withdrawing, they spoke with one another, saying, This man does nothing worthy of death or of bonds.

It is of interest here that the Jews clearly thought that Paul said or done something wrong, worthy of death because that is why they brought him to trial. The problem was that Paul broke a Jewish religious law and not a Roman law. The Jews thought that Paul was worthy of stoning for he violated an aspect of their religion, their most important world view. The Romans did not think that Paul deserved death because the charge was related to a sub-group of the four world views rather than the major world view of politics. It is also interesting to note that the Romans viewed the Jewish religious laws as Jewish that did not concern them. Yet, any view or action of the Jews related to politics were not seen by the Romans as Jewish politics, which did not concern them, but they regarded it as their politics, prompting swift action. Politics were more important to the Romans than any of the other world views.

An interesting case was recorded in Acts 16: A young women with an evil spirit followed Paul for days. She also kept on shouting as she trailed him. After a few days Paul could not take it any longer and expelled the spirit. This infuriated her owners, however, as she could no longer tell people's fortunes to earn an income. It is important to note that Paul did nothing wrong; all he did was to evict an evil spirit, which is actually a religious matter with economic consequences. How were the owners to convince a Roman judge to convict Paul over a religious matter when the Romans are only concerned about political issues?

> *Acts 16:19-22 When her owners realized that their chance of making money was gone, they seized Paul and Silas and dragged them to the authorities in the public square. They brought them before the Roman officials and said, "These men are Jews, and they are causing trouble in our city. They are teaching customs that are against our law; we are Roman citizens, and we cannot accept these customs or practice them."*

To obtain a Roman conviction they had to bring charges which a Roman judge would find relevant. Since the Romans felt so strongly about politics they had to bring political charges – even though this case had nothing to do with politics for a New Testament Jew. They knew, however, that the Roman authorities hated and reacted powerfully against trouble, uprisings, riots, etc., in cities, so, they accused Paul and Silas of "causing trouble in our city" and teaching and practicing wrong customs, breaking the Roman law. Now, Paul did nothing of the sort, but the accusers knew that this was the only way to obtain a conviction because of the Roman world view.

The people knew full well that if they wanted to get the attention of the Romans religion was not the answer, but political unrest was. The Jews reacted against Jesus, as well as against the disciples and the apostles, because of religious reasons, but because of the Roman's overarching view of politics they had to use public unrest to get them into trouble.

Acts 17:5 But some Jews were jealous and gathered worthless loafers from the streets and formed a mob. They set the whole city in an uproar and attacked the home of a man named Jason, in an attempt to find Paul and Silas and bring them out to the people.

The villains orchestrated this riot deliberately when there was no accepted reason from Paul's words or actions for such a riot. They arranged the demonstration because they knew they needed it to cause trouble for Paul and Silas with the Romans. Not only did they cause a riot, but they also needed some political charge against Paul and Silas. It is interesting to look at the charge, with which they accused Paul and Silas:

Acts 17:7-8 "... They are all breaking the laws of the Emperor, saying that there is another king, whose name is Jesus." With these words they threw the crowd and the city authorities in an uproar.

The Roman law in question is not acknowledging "another king". As anticipated, this certainly got the authority's attention as it touched a political nerve. The interesting thing is that Paul did not call Jesus "King" anywhere in the entire book of acts. The accusers brought these charges specifically because of the anticipated reaction they knew Rome would have.

On another occasion Paul understood which world view was the most important to which group: He knew that the Pharisees were concerned about the religious law, while the Sadducees were involved with the temple and its religious sacrifices, and that the Romans were concerned about politics. Thus, Paul wove the Roman law, the temple and Roman politics into his defense to reply to the specific objections each group had against him.

Act 25:8 Defending himself, Paul said, Neither against the Law of the Jews, nor against the temple, nor against Caesar have I offended in anything.

Jesus' reign was referred to in the book of Acts. It was also brought up in the events of His own trial. Notice how the Jews never accused Jesus Himself of breaking Roman laws; they accused Him only of religious offences. They had to do this to obtain a verdict of guilt from the Jews before they could take Jesus to the Romans. Yet, when dealing with the Romans, the Jews quickly brought political charges against Him with no word about any religious matters. They had to change the charges as they knew that the only way to obtain a verdict of guilt from the Romans would be if the charges related to politics, rather than to religion.

After reading the gospels and looking at the topics over which they fought with Jesus, religious authority, blasphemy, religious law, the temple, religious doctrine, etc., one almost gasps, hearing the actual charges brought against Jesus when brought before the Romans. One cannot but ask: "Where did those come from …?" The invented sins of Jesus were not presented to the Romans as the topics with which the Jews grappled with Jesus: No, instead they accused Jesus of political transgression before the Romans:

Luke 23:2 And they began to accuse Him, saying, We have found this one perverting the nation and forbidding them to give tribute to Caesar, saying himself to be a king, Christ.

The Jews forgot conveniently that they had a discussion with Jesus about this very topic. They forgot Jesus' answer to their question about tax to Caesar. Jesus did not forbid anyone in any way to render tribute to Caesar. In fact, Jesus said the opposite:

Matt 22:17-21 Therefore tell us; what do you think? Is it lawful to give tribute to Caesar or not? But Jesus perceived their wickedness, and said, Why do you tempt Me, hypocrites? Show Me the tribute money. And they brought a denarius to Him. And He said to them, Whose image and inscription is this? They said to Him, Caesar's. Then He said to them, Therefore render to Caesar the things that are Caesar's, and to God the things which are God's.

The Jews knew very well that to Romans politics were the ultimate concern. Not only did they play the political card, but used it effectively to turn the screws even tighter. They reasoned that if Pilate would release Jesus, they would be able to get him into political trouble with his ultimate authority, Caesar.

John 19:12 From this time, Pilate sought to release Him. But the Jews cried out, saying, If you let this man go, you are not Caesar's friend. Whoever makes himself a king speaks against Caesar.

It is amazing that the Jews hated Jesus so much, which was not the case with the Zealots, and that they viewed their religious purposes so much higher than any political purposes that they were willing to sacrifice politics to gain religious points. In order to deal with Jesus – a religious problem - they sacrificed their politics, or rather their anti-Roman politics, when claiming Caesar as their king:

John 19:15 But they cried out, Away with him! Away with him! Crucify him! Pilate said to them, Shall I crucify your king? The chief priests answered, We have no king but Caesar.

It seems as if the Jews developed this plan earlier to accuse Jesus politically: The Pharisees held a meeting to develop a strategy against Jesus; this strategy was specifically designed to be appealing to, and effective with, the Romans. The strategic design was evident in the words with which they attempted to entrap Jesus and the people they used as witnesses. The context of asking Jesus the question of paying tribute to Caesar is as follows:

Matt 22:15-17 Then the Pharisees left and took counsel that they might entangle Him in words.   And they sent their disciples out to Him along with the Herodians, saying, Master, we know that you are true, and that you teach the way of God in truth. Nor do you care for anyone, for you do not regard the person of men. Therefore tell us; what do you think? Is it lawful to give tribute to Caesar or not?

75

Firstly, also the Herodians were sent to Jesus. The Herodians were a political group, aligned with King Herod Antipas. If Jesus would speak out against Caesar they were going to take Jesus to the Roman authorities, and if they would fail the Herodians would certainly take care of delivering the message to the appropriate Roman powers.

Secondly, the preamble to the main question seems intended to pressure Jesus to give the answer they wished for. The preamble urges Jesus to speak God's truth and not to consider any person in his answer; of course, the Pharisees had a specific person in mind – Caesar. In short, they were basically instructing Jesus to answer the question definitely in the negative; not to pay taxes. They thought that if Jesus would answer, "no", they would have a case that would get the Romans especially interested, and rapidly. Even after Jesus said, "pay unto Caesar what is Caesar's", they still accused Him of forbidding them to give tribute or tax to Caesar.

This game was played politically, even though their issue with Jesus was a religious concern; there was just no other way to obtain a verdict of guilt from the Romans.

Luke 20:20 And they watched and sent forth spies, pretending themselves to be righteous men, so that they might seize upon a word of His, that they might deliver Him in this way to the power and authority of the governor.

In conclusion, the Jewish world view was that all components of society were dominated, formed and shaped by religion. The Roman world view denied the Jewish world view and, alternatively, situated politics at the center of everything. These opposing world views clashed sometimes. Yet, at other times, the Jews used the Roman world view when dealing with Rome to achieve their religious desires. Similarly, the Romans used religion to gain favors from the Jews. The Jews not only knew how to use politics with the Romans, but also knew when Roman politics would defeat their purposes. During the time leading up to Jesus' arrest the religious leaders planned the timing of the seizure deliberately to minimize Roman political reaction to a possible uproar. A political uproar at this time would have taken the focus off Jesus and they wished to place it later on a more significant and important audience, the rioters:

Matt 26:4-5 And they consulted so that they might take Jesus by guile and kill Him. But they said, not on the feast day, lest there be an uproar among the people.

The "chess match" between using religion with the Jews and politics with the Romans is strikingly evident in Jesus' arrest, trial and crucifixion. In front of the Sanhedrin, as per Jewish custom, the accusations were of a religious nature. In fact, the accusation is even tailored to the Sanhedrin's soft spot; the temple. The accusations were false, and since they were not true they could have made up any accusation of their choice. So, why then did they choose a religious charge? This trial was before a Jewish group to which religion was supreme.

Matt 26:60-61 But they found none; yea, though many false witnesses came, they found none. But at last two false witnesses came up and said, This one said, I am able to destroy the temple of God and to build it in three days.

Jesus was questioned as they were looking for more and even more persuasive religious reasons. The first charges were very compelling, but only to the Sadducees. They had to find a charge therefore, uniting the Sadducees, Pharisees, Essenes and Zealots, and that charge was blasphemy.

Matt 26:65 Then the high priest tore his clothes, saying, He has spoken blasphemy! What further need do we have of witnesses? Behold, now you have heard his blasphemy.

Once again, we find a religious charge in front of a religious group. The Romans would have laughed at this charge since they thought there were many gods anyway and even if it breached some Jewish religious law, it did not concern them, as it was not a political threat. So, these charges, founding Jesus guilty, were useless to convict Jesus by the Romans. It is vital to note that the charges against Jesus brought before the Sanhedrin, destroying God's temple and blasphemy, were the grounds upon which they decided to have Jesus killed

(Matt 26:66), but these disappeared before Pilate. The Bible text is repeated here:

> *Luke 23:1-2 And rising up, all the multitude of them led Him before Pilate. And they began to accuse Him, saying, We have found this one perverting the nation and forbidding them to give tribute to Caesar, saying himself to be a king, Christ.*

As with the charges brought to the Sanhedrin these charges were clearly false. Jesus already answered to this question before, and testified to Caesar's reign and the payment of taxes to Caesar. Being false charges, they could have come up with any charge of their choice, so, why produce this particular charge? They chose it as they knew the Roman mind; they knew that politics was vital to the Romans and they had to lay a charge of this nature to find Jesus guilty in a Roman court. A potential uproar or political unrest was the final persuasion Pilate needed to take action. It seems as if Pilate's action was motivated only by the avoidance of political consequences. Upheavals and riots would have been a clear signal to Caesar that Pilate was an incompetent ruler. The political consequences were clear.

> *Matt 27:24 But when Pilate saw that it gained nothing, but rather that an uproar was made, he took water and washed his hands before the crowd, saying, I am innocent of the blood of this just person. You see to it.*

The Jewish view of religious dominion over politics, economics and kinship, and the Roman view that politics dominated religion, economics and kinship came out strikingly in the conversation between Pilate and Jesus. Pilate is amazed that Jesus is not defending Himself, so Pilate advances his political authority as the reason why Jesus should speak up.

> *John 19:10 Then Pilate said to him, Do you not speak to me? Do you not know that I have authority to crucify you, and I have authority to release you?*

Jesus' reason for not speaking up, however, is not based upon political authority, which, according to Jesus did not exist, for authority came from God – thereby making it a religious matter rather than a political matter. Furthermore, Jesus viewed this trial as a sin of those who caused it, that is actually as a religious matter; to the Romans, however, it was a political matter.

John 19:11 Jesus answered, You could have no authority against Me unless it were given to you from above. Therefore he who delivered Me to you has the greater sin.

Jesus' view was that political authority was reserved for unbelievers or pagans. Jews, including religious believers, were supposed to substitute political authority with religious service. Religion, according to Jesus, was supreme as it was more important than politics.

Luke 22:24-26 And there was also a dispute among them as to which of them seems to be greater. And He said to them, The kings of the nations exercise lordship over them. And they who exercise authority on them are called benefactors. But you shall not be so: but the greater among you, let him be as the lesser, and he who governs, as one who serves.

Just for interest's sake, most of the Western world today subscribe to a world view dominated by the economy. The political vote is determined by people's belief how their votes are going to influence their finances. People raise their children, kinship, with the best education possible and guide them to choose careers based on expected income and an economic standing in the future. Faith in Christ is often shelved as the economy, possession and lifestyle become their gods. Thus the modern Western world view seems to reflect the following scenario:

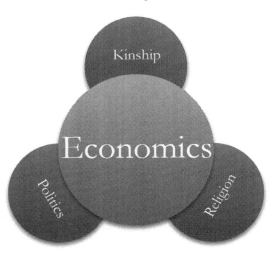

There are certainly many more tools available and necessary for unlocking the secrets of New Testament stories in a better way. For the stories addressed in part two, however, these four tools will suffice. In case other explanations are necessary they will be provided in the discussion of the story in question. It is hoped that these tools would be used to unlock the secrets of even more stories in future as they are applicable to other stories, not treated here. The four tools, discussed above, which have provided the social context[67] for the stories discussed here, are the following:

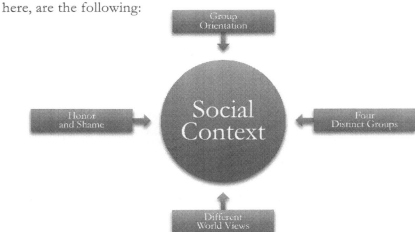

---

[67] There are many other tools and background information that supply the context. The four presented here are by no means exhaustive, but rather a starting point to provide a partial indication of, or peek at, how the New Testament audience may have understood Jesus' stories.

It is important to note that these four tools are only four elements, comprising the broader social context of the New Testament stories. Many more elements make up the social context, but they will not be discussed here.

PART II: Unlocking the Secrets of Jesus' Stories

❧ CHAPTER SEVEN ❧

THE HEALING OF THE PARALYTIC

Matt 9:1-7; Mark 2:1-12; Luke 5:17-26

The story of the paralytic began with some men bringing him to Jesus on a mat. In a group-oriented society this is rather strange. Society saw an ill person as being temporarily punished by God for sins. In this society the cause of the illness could be either because of the sins of the sick person, or the sins of the person's group, usually his family. Either way, since illness was viewed as temporary, the cause of the illness or sins was not too bad. On the vertical line of social status ill people fell below the acceptable line into the "sinner's" category; therefore, these people were rejected.

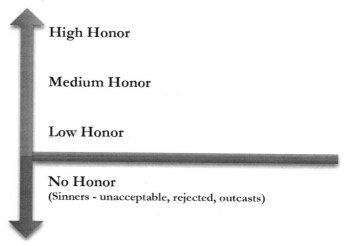

High Honor

Medium Honor

Low Honor

No Honor
(Sinners - unacceptable, rejected, outcasts)

In the case of a disabled person the social rejection was much worse, for disabilities were permanent. According to society's view this meant that God's punishment was more severe and, therefore, the sins for which the punishment was intended, were also more severe. Disabilities were regarded as the liability of the disabled persons or their group, usually their parents. Consequently, disabled people fell below ill people in the "sinner's" category.

Once people were classified as "sinners", honorable people did not wish to have anything to do with them. After all, if a sinner was assisted, this support was interpreted as working against God. Alms-giving were permitted to disabled people, but that was about all.

Acts 3:2 And a certain man, who was lame from his mother's womb, was being carried. And they laid him daily at that temple gate which is called Beautiful, to ask alms from those who entered into the temple.

The question concerning this particular paralytic man's mode of transportation, "carrying him", was, "Why were these men bringing the paralytic?" No one was supposed to assist disabled people. By assisting this sinner their status would immediately drop from honorable to shameful. New Testament society would have raised their eyebrows because no healthy people, with some level of honor, were freely associating themselves with a disabled person with no honor. Association between people had an impact on their own honor. In this case the healthy people were simply throwing away their honor.

Secondly, these people would have been considered as acting against God. They would be cast out of their groups, and in a group-oriented society that would have been the end of any kind of decent life. Why were they willing to risk everything to assist this man? Why were they throwing away their own lives? As can be expected, for this very reason, there were clear cases of "sinners" not having anybody to assist them:

John 5:7 The infirm man answered Him, Sir, when the water is troubled, I have no one to put me into the pool. But while I am coming, another steps down before me.

A logical conclusion could be that the helpers were from the same social group as the man they supported. Perhaps they were also outcasts. They must have had lost their honor already. They must have been classified already as "sinners" themselves. This must have been the only[68] reason why they would be willing to aid this man – they had nothing to lose – they had lost everything already. The exception was that family members would help family members; however, as we have already seen, such family members already shared the same status as the sick or disabled persons; they were sometimes even blamed for the disability. Thus, they did not have anything more to lose either. There is a great deal of evidence to support the fact that the ill and disabled formed their own groups, albeit groups with no status.

Luke 17:12 And as He entered into a certain village, ten leprous men met Him, who stood afar off.

In other examples where people assisted the disabled we also found that the helpers had left their previous groups prior to being willing to assist. Typically, they joined lower status groups because they were expelled from their higher status groups, or because of their newly found faith, which clearly taught them that the esteem of humans was not important, but only God's view mattered. Thus, we find a clear example in the book of Acts:

Acts 5:13-15 And of the rest no one dared to join himself to them, but the people magnified them; and more believing ones were added to the Lord, multitudes both of men and women; So as to carry out the sick into the streets and place them on cots and mattresses, so that at least the shadow of Peter passing by might overshadow some of them.

Here we found believers being "added to" the Lord. That also meant that they had been removed from their groups and then joined the Lord's group. To begin with, Christians were viewed as a low status group. Once being part of this new group, they were willing to assist

---

[68] This is most likely assuming these men were Jews. Of course, if these men were non-Jews and from a totally different culture honor and shame may not have played a big role to them.

other people with no status. There is also another example of people aiding the disabled, found in Mark 6:55-56. This event took place at Gennesaret, which was North-East of the Sea of Galilee. The Jewish influence might not have been so great here and their culture was very different. We knew this because this was where Jesus had given permission for the demons to enter into the herd of pigs. After the masses of pigs had drowned the city was dissatisfied with Jesus. In fact, they begged Him to leave their area.

Mark 5:17 And they began to beg Him to leave their borders.

It was not legal for Jews to own pig herds, nor had they any use for them. They would not have been upset with Jesus about what happened there. It was obvious, therefore, that these people were non-Jews and hence, from a different culture.

In any event, returning to the paralytic, the men who brought him to Jesus for healing must have been "sinners" too. This man was a paralytic and in society's view he was sinful, dishonorable and unacceptable; he was a "reject".

By the way, rejection may very well be the reason why most ill and disabled people's names were not provided. They were nameless, nonentities and "nobodies"; and when such an insignificant person's name was revealed we discovered that the person's very name often revealed and confirmed his or her status as a nonentity or a "nobody".

Mark 10:46 And they came to Jericho. And as He with His disciples and a large crowd went out of Jericho, blind Bartimeus, the son of Timeus, was sitting by the side of the highway, begging.

Apparently, this blind man's name was known, but interestingly, as has been mentioned before, the word *"bar"* meant "son of...", which indicated that this man's name simply signified "son of Timeus". In other words, he was looked upon as so worthless that he did not even receive his *own* name. He came to be known as the son of his father. In the case of Barabbas not even his father's name is mentioned. So, we have seen that people who were classified as "sinners" lost their identity; they were indeed "nobodies". The paralytic in our base texts, (Matt 9:1-7; Mark 2:1-12; Luke 5:17-26), is no exception to this rule, for he too was nameless. He was only known by his disability. *His disability became his name.* Jesus saw the faith of the four people bringing the paralytic to Him and said to the paralytic:

Matt 9:2 ... Child, be of good cheer. Your sins are forgiven you.

Now, why would Jesus say, "Your sins are forgiven", rather than just healing this person physically? Would this not be an indication that Jesus concurred with society that this person was a paralytic because of his sins? It seems as though there was evidence to suggest that Jesus did in fact agree with society and that sin led to God's punishment.

John 5:14 Afterward Jesus found him in the temple and said to him, Behold, you are made whole. Sin no more lest a worse thing come to you.

The man in John's account in this text was not described with a disability, but with an infirmity. In this case it might have been that this man's illness was self-inflicted by some sinful or careless behavior; recurrence of such behavior would naturally result in the reappearance of the illness. Perhaps he had a bad habit, which had the same results as smoking causing lung cancer, or drinking alcohol causing liver disease. If this was the case, Jesus' comment made sense; this was probably the case as we know that Jesus did not believe that sins brought about disabilities or illnesses unrelated to the sinful action itself. The illness or disability could be brought on by God, however, but for a different reason, as was disclosed by Jesus at a different occasion when the disciples asked Him this question directly:

John 9:2-3 And His disciples asked Him, saying, Master, who sinned, this man or his parents, that he was born blind? Jesus answered, neither has this man nor his parents sinned, but that the works of God might be revealed in him.

So, if Jesus did not believe that disability resulted from the sins of the disabled, or from the parents, why would Jesus say the paralytic' sins were forgiven? Furthermore, Jesus knew that the Pharisees were present when He said, "Your sins are forgiven." He knew that the

Pharisees were regarded as the keepers and interpreters of the law. Jesus knew this would cause a stir, but He still said it. By Jesus' own admission He could have said something else:

> *Matt 9:5 For which is easier? To say, Your sins are forgiven you, or to say, Arise and walk!*

Jesus may have had two reasons for choosing the former option, namely, "Your sins are forgiven": Firstly, the obvious reason inherent in the text was to demonstrate that He had the authority to do so:

> *Matt 9:6 But so that you may know that the Son of Man has authority on earth to forgive sins, then He said to the paralytic, Arise, take up your bed and go to your house.*

The religious leaders assumed their authority automatically[69]. Their involvement in the temple was a testimony of their authority. According to them Jesus had no authority, and whatever authority Jesus did have, was ruled as illegitimate authority; Jesus refuted that ruling here.

Secondly, Jesus wanted to state publically that the paralytic's sins were forgiven for a subtle, yet profound reason, which is only apparent once this story is cast in the group-oriented society in which it took place, and if one understands the dynamics of honor and shame present in such a society. If we would use the tools in part one, they would unlock a secret about this story that demonstrated Jesus' compassion, His desire not only to heal this person, *but to restore him.*

Yes, Jesus could have simply healed him and said, "Arise and walk"; but such a healing would have been a physical healing only. Once healed, he would still have been a "nonentity", even though he would have been a "nobody" with a healthy body. He would still have been classified as someone with no honor. He would still belong to the same group and share the same level of dishonor with them. At best his honor may have increased by a fraction only. He would have risen above the disabled and above the sick, but he would have been still below the coveted acceptable line of demarcation. Jesus did not desire that for this

---

[69] Driggers 2007:241.

man. Jesus did not wish to heal him physically *only*, albeit a wonderful gift! Jesus wanted this man to be fully restored, both physically and socially. He did not only want to give this man health, He also wanted to give him life; quality of life. Quality of life in this society can only be achieved with acceptance by society and the honor associated with such acceptance. There was only one way for Jesus to accomplish this feat: To restore him in the eyes of this group-oriented, status-sensitive, honor- and shame-driven society.

Jesus had to pronounce this man free from God's judgment and punishment. For if God forgave him, who could still hold anything against him? Even though Jesus did not believe that this man was a paralytic because of individual or of a group's sin, society believed that[70]; He wanted society to forgive this man too, because God forgave him. Jesus knew that they did not wish to assist sinners because of fear of working against God and of shame as a result of association with the dishonorable. Jesus used that same view to protect this man from social injustice. Jesus' logic followed this line of thinking: If people did not wish to go against God by assisting sinners, then they could not go against God by forgiving this man if God forgave him. Jesus used their world view of religion, being the supreme value above all other components of society, to accomplish this task. He used religion to fix kinship and relationships.

Jesus cared so much for this man that He was willing to risk another confrontation with the Pharisees. He was willing to risk being rejected by society for blasphemy just to restore this man fully. Jesus was willing to lose honor so that the paralytic may gain honor. Jesus provided the paralytic with physical healing, but He also bestowed him

---

[70] Please note that we are not talking about the accumulative effect of sin as a whole, resulting in general degeneration since Adam's sin. Jesus did not believe that individual sins were directly and immediately punished by God. It is not the purpose here to address the topic of God's actions relating to people's sins. Suffice it to say that God does sometimes act on a person due to their sins, like Miriam; Moses' sister. Generally though, the person involved knew what they were doing was wrong, was typically warned, and still chose to go ahead with their wrong deed. Furthermore, the Old Testament Hebrew culture attributed just about everything to God because they did not see Satan as an autonomous being. For example, in the beginning of the book of Job it states that Satan ruined Job's life, but in the last chapter it says that God did all these things to him. To some extent Jesus came to correct this view and to vindicate God's character.

with honor. What a Savior! The paralytic and his friends came only for physical healing, but Jesus also granted him what he did not even ask for, what he probably thought might not even be possible: His healing of being a person of shame to becoming a person with honor. Jesus said, "Your sins are forgiven", to remove all blame and judgment. Jesus removed the reason for societal rejection and restored his place in society: Jesus furnished him with health and honor.

✃ CHAPTER EIGHT ✄

THE MAN WITH LEPROSY

Matt 8:1-4; Mark 1:40-45; Luke 5:12-16

Jesus often exhibited the complete healing of the body and the providing of all human needs. One such an occasion was when a leprous person came and knelt before Jesus for healing. Leprosy was seen as a symbol of death and leprous people were described as "walking tombs"; and they were expelled from other people, camps, towns, and any gathering of people. Specific laws governed this disease:

> *Lev 14:2 This shall be the law of the leper in the day of his cleansing.*

Lepers had to keep their distance. Not only were lepers ordered to keep their distance, but people naturally withdrew physically from them for fear of contracting the disease. Lepers had to warn others of their presence by calling out, "unclean, unclean!"

> *Lev 13:45-46 And as for the leper in whom the plague is, his clothes shall be torn, and his head shall be bare, and he shall put a covering on his upper lip, and shall cry, Unclean! Unclean! All the days in which the plague is in him he shall be defiled. He is unclean. He shall live alone. His dwelling shall be outside the camp.*

Leviticus 13 and 14 explained in great detail how people had to exert themselves to isolate lepers. Lepers were to stay at least fifty paces away from other people. Provision was also made in these chapters for the re-admission to society of people who had been found to be cured; but when a person was viewed as unclean they were regarded as no better than a pig. They were not good enough to be considered worthy of personhood.

As we have seen already, leprosy meant immediate dishonor and a loss of all social standing and privilege. We have also discovered that it indicated religious problems of sinfulness to the New Testament Jewish mindset. Just as leprosy was deemed to be contagious physically it was similarly seen as to be contagious spiritually and socially. Consequently, nobody wanted anything to do with lepers.

This particular leper showed a flagrant disregard for the rules of society: What was he doing kneeling right in front of Jesus when he was supposed to be some fifty paces away? Why was he speaking to Jesus when he was supposed to call out "unclean, unclean!"? Surely he should have been stoned for breaking the law and putting everyone else in danger of physical illness and spiritual corruption. We have to remember that a group-oriented society was used to sacrificing an individual for the benefit of the group.

Perhaps this man felt the burden of leprosy and its consequences too hard to bear. Maybe he felt as if he had nothing to lose: Yes, he could have lost his life, but what kind of life was it anyway? Perhaps his illness had progressed to such an extent that he was close to death in any case. He may have seen this opportunity as an all-or-nothing gamble with everything to gain and not a great deal to lose; everything that mattered had already been lost. There seems to be a hint of a paradox in this man's actions: On the one hand, he wished to be healed; healing meant readmission into the group. Yet, on the other hand, his actions disregarded the group. His very actions would have influenced the group to disregard him. In other words, he indirectly asked for readmission into the group with an action which would have resulted in isolation.

This nameless leprous man's actions, however, showed that he knew his position in life, for he knelt before Jesus. Kneeling and lowering of the body indicated an acknowledgement of lesser status than the person before whom one kneels. The way in which this man asked for healing also showed respect for Jesus as his request leaves room for Jesus to decline the request gracefully.

Matt 8:2   And behold, a leper came and worshiped him, saying, Lord, if You will, You can make me clean.

As we have seen in the previous story Jesus did not only wish to heal a person physically, but also wanted to satisfy the human need of acceptance, of being loved, and so forth. Jesus could have just healed this person physically and sent him on his way, but Jesus knew his heart better than he himself: Jesus knew his desire for acceptance. Jesus felt empathy for this person. Perhaps Jesus placed Himself imaginarily in this man's position by asking Himself how He would have felt if He were the leper. Mark told us that Jesus was "moved with compassion"; then, especially if it were Jesus, He would not do just the minimum.

How could Jesus demonstrate His compassion? How could Jesus accept him noticeably? In which way could Jesus exhibit practical acceptance for others to see so that they might be moved to do the same? In the previous story Jesus forgave the paralytic's sins to indicate God's approval. Here Jesus did the unthinkable:

Matt 8:3   And Jesus put out His hand and touched him, saying, I will; be clean! And immediately his leprosy was cleansed.

Jesus touched the untouchable and accepted the rejected. Jesus humanized the anonymous. Jesus fulfilled the desire of the leper's heart. In the eyes of New Testament Jews Jesus risked his personal health and spiritual well-being, and that for an undeserving, law-breaking sinner. Jesus, however, did not wish to leave this man as a law breaker. He commanded the leper to follow the law by showing himself to the priest for inspection. He was also instructed not to tell anybody about the manner of his healing. Luke told us that Jesus had instructed the man "sternly". The reason for this man's previous non-compliance was apparent in Luke's account as Jesus was not able to enter the cities; perhaps there was a pattern of non-compliance here. There might have been a possible second reason why Jesus told him not to speak out: As before, the reason might have been buried in the larger context of the gospels:

For this man to be re-admitted into society he had to be cleared by the priests. Priests were mostly Sadducees and they clashed with Jesus all the time. If the leper would have told them that it was Jesus who cleansed him they might not have declared him clean, as such a clearance would have been an acknowledgement of Jesus' authority and power over illness and sin; this was something they would not have been willing to do. The end result might have been physical healing without re-admittance into society; a job half-done. Jesus, however, showed concern for this man's well-being. He was willing to bury the glory He was worthy of so that this man could be raised to life.

It had to be assumed that he had shown himself to the priests prior to broadcasting his story for all to hear. This assumption was based on the fact that he went out and "proclaimed" and "spread" the news. He, however, would not have been allowed to "go out" and proclaim it if he had not yet been declared clean. The fact that he did so presupposed his clearance.

Jesus always puts us, as people in need, first; He thinks about the best for us. He accepts us no matter what our condition may be, and He never leaves our healing half-done.

❧ CHAPTER NINE ❦

THE MAN WITH A WITHERED HAND

Matt 12:9-13; Mark 3:1-6; Luke 6:6-11

One day Jesus and His disciples walked through a grain field. They were hungry, but had nothing to eat except the grain growing next to them. They did what was logical to do and plucked some grain. So far everything went well apart from one small detail: It was done on the Sabbath. As this action was deemed as "harvesting on the Sabbath" it qualified as law-breaking.

The main group concerned with the law in New Testament times was the Pharisees. This event certainly disturbed them a great deal. They accused Jesus and His disciples promptly of breaking the Sabbath.

It was in the context of this accusation that both Jesus and the Pharisees wished to put forward their case. The Pharisees wished to nail Jesus on the issue of what was legal to do on the Sabbath and what was not. Jesus wished to present His case of human care. Jesus wished them to comprehend that the Sabbath was an opportunity to do good. With both sides wishing to prove their points of view, a showdown was looming.

Conceivably, Jesus went to the Synagogue to settle this matter: He entered their domain; this was where they were in control; this was where they taught. Mark and Luke informed us that Jesus did the probing questioning. According to Matthew, however, the Pharisees questioned Jesus. Perhaps this disparity demonstrated the battle between

Jesus and the Pharisees. One could clearly see the tussle going back and forth in the text; it is not surprising that they were not sure of who was leading what discussion. Either way the intent was very apparent.

> *Matt 12:10 And behold, a man having a withered hand. And they asked Him, saying, is it lawful to heal on the Sabbaths? This so that they might accuse Him.*

What was this man with the withered hand doing in the synagogue? There were some cases in the New Testament where people with health issues were found in the synagogue. On the other hand, religious leaders often used banishment from the synagogue as punishment. Having a withered hand makes this man a sinner. Having a withered hand made him liable to be punished by God. Having a withered hand, made the Pharisees wanting to assist God in His punishment of the sinner such as banishment from the synagogue. There were certainly discussions in the New Testament of religious leaders banning people from the synagogue. Being banned from the synagogue resulted in shame. Here, we had yet another example of religion being used to control kinship.

> *John 9:22 His parents spoke these things because they feared the Jews, for the Jews had already agreed that if anyone confessed that He was Christ, he should be put out of the synagogue.*

> *John 12:42 Still, however, even out of the rulers, many did believe on Him. But because of the Pharisees they did not confess, lest they should be put out of the synagogue.*

This man might possibly have been in the synagogue by invitation from the Pharisees because they knew Jesus would have wished to heal him. He might have been placed there as a temptation for Jesus to break their law, since it was still Sabbath. They wished to catch Jesus breaking the law here in the synagogue where witnesses were present, rather than being satisfied with what just happened in the field where perhaps only the Pharisees saw Him "transgressing the law". The Pharisees knew Jesus healed people wherever He went. They knew that Jesus would take the trap set for Him and heal this person. It was interesting what this taught us about who Jesus was and how much He cared for those who suffered.

Before we continue it has to be stated that Jesus never broke God's moral law:

2 Cor 5:21 For He has made Him who knew no sin, to be sin for us, that we might become the righteousness of God in Him.

1 Pet 2:22 He who did no sin, nor was guile found in His mouth.

The Pharisees did not only believe and live according to the Mosaic Law, but they also believed and taught according to the "tradition of the elders". The tradition of the elders was a commentary or interpretation of the Mosaic Law as transmitted and expanded on over centuries. These commentaries were actually codified. The Pharisees believed that these commentaries were valid and had to be obeyed. They also referred to these traditions as "laws" or "the law". When they accused Jesus of breaking "the law" they were actually referred to the traditional interpretation of the law. Modern readers often thought that Jesus broke the Sabbath law as written in the Ten Commandments, but He did not. Jesus only broke their interpretation and their rules with regard to Sabbath-keeping. We have already referred to one interpretation of such a law – the Sabbath day's journey. These laws were often called "legalistic laws" as the Pharisees believed that if everybody kept all of these laws perfectly well for one or two Sabbaths they would legally be reconciled to God and then the Messiah would come.

"Jews will be redeemed by virtue of their Sabbath observance. (Hiyya ben Abba." Leviticus Rabbah 3.1)

"If Israel kept properly one Sabbath, the Son of David would come, for Sabbath is equivalent to all other commandments." (Levi. Exodus Rabbah 25.12)

"If Israel observed properly two Sabbaths, they would be redeemed immediately." (Simeon ben Yohai. Talmud: Shabbat 118b)

This was why the Pharisees became the "Sabbath police". They confronted anyone who broke the Sabbath law. This was why they took great offense when someone broke the Sabbath law. After all, the person breaking the Sabbath law was responsible for the Messiah's delay. Breaking the Sabbath law was bad enough, but teaching and instructing others to break the Sabbath law was incomprehensible; and this was what they believed Jesus had done. Now, they were seeking definitive proof in their synagogue with a direct question and an enticing temptation as the man with the withered hand looked on.

The trap they set for Jesus here was not based on the Mosaic Law, but rather based on their laws which they referred to as the "tradition of the elders". This tradition in fact did provide for medical attention on the Sabbath, but such attention was limited to situations where people were either in danger of losing their lives, or experiencing pain.

"Saving a life supersedes the Sabbath." *(Eleazar ben Azariah. Mekilta to Exodus 31.13)*

"No Sabbath laws apply where life is in danger." *(Mathia ben Heresh, Mishna: Yoma 8:6)*

"To save a life, disregard a Sabbath, that the endangered may enjoy many Sabbaths." *(Simeon ben Menasya. Talmud: Yoma 85b)*

"You may violate the Sabbath to relieve pain." *(Matia ben Heresh. Talmud: Yoma 84a)*

Based upon all these traditions the Pharisees would expect any Jew to agree with them that it was not lawful to heal on the Sabbath where there is no danger of loss of life, or painful suffering. Healing the man with the withered hand would have been constituted as "Sabbath breaking", according to their tradition, because this man's life was not in danger and neither did he have any pain. He might have been this way for many years. The healing could have waited easily for one more day; the withered hand did not present any urgency for immediate care. The Pharisees wanted Jesus to comply with these traditions as they were regarded as more than just traditions: They were looked upon as laws; but Jesus' responded strangely:

Matt 12:11   And He said to them, What man among you will be, who will have one sheep, and if it falls into a pit on the Sabbaths, will he not lay hold on it and lift it out?

The Pharisees thought that they had every angle covered. They had all the quotes stating clearly that medical help could only be rendered when a person suffered pain, or was in danger. Brilliant Jesus! He too quoted from their traditions. Their traditions stated that sustenance was to be provided for animals, having fallen into cisterns or pits. At nightfall the animals could be rescued. If, however, the animals were in danger of not surviving the day, tools, for example, mattresses were permitted to be carried out and used to save the animals. (Shab. 128a; "Yad," Shabbat, xxv:26; Oraḥ Ḥayyim, 305:19) It should be noted that this was a controversial issue: The rules concerning this issue was constantly changed and they were still not settled a hundred years after Matthew's writing.

Jesus was probably aware of the existence of different opinions concerning these traditions; therefore, His counter quote was in the form of a question rather than an emphatic statement. It was also interesting to note that Jesus put the question in the negative, "*not* lay hold". Thus, Jesus was asking whether anyone did not agree with His understanding of the tradition. Since the Pharisees did not object to the question, or raised a controversy over it, and since the question was asked in such a way as to solicit disagreement, it might be assumed that they agreed with it.

By foregoing to answer Jesus' question and thereby consenting to its conclusion, the Pharisees now faced an unspoken but simple follow-up question: If you were willing to assist the animal, why were you unwilling to assist the man with the withered hand? We have to remember that the Pharisees were experts in Mosaic law. They were used to dissecting it, separating emotion from it and majoring in the *minutiae,* small and trivial details. In this particular case they could still point to the fact that the man with the withered hand was not in danger of losing his life, nor was he in pain.

Jesus did not debate this particular case; He did not speak about the disabled man: Instead, He questioned their traditions: He was judging their legal religious system. He pointed out how merciless and unfair their system was in making provision for an animal, but not for a human being. Jesus put their law on trial and demonstrated that their law elevated animals above humans. Now, Jesus reversed their hierarchy:

Matt 12:12 How much better is a man then than a sheep? Therefore it is lawful to do well on the Sabbath days.

By this statement Jesus defied the Pharisaic law, and indirectly the Pharisees themselves. Jesus' statement was both categorical and clear-cut, as well as positive. Being put so positively made it almost impossible to argue against His contention; who was going to say that it was not lawful to do well on the Sabbath? Jesus renders their law a joke. Jesus' logic indicated, if it was lawful to assist an animal without its life being in danger, and a human being was worth more than an animal, then surely, it ought to be also lawful to assist the human being.

Jesus knew that this was a trap. The critical and judgmental eyes of the Pharisees proclaimed loud and clear that this was a test. The only way for Jesus not to fall into this trap, however, was for the man with the withered hand not to be healed. Jesus has never been known for placing His own interests above the interests of others. Jesus cared a great deal for those who suffered; this man certainly suffered socially as a reject. He would rather expose Himself to trouble than letting the suffering continue.

By now the Pharisees probably knew that Jesus was going to disregard them and their laws. They knew that Jesus was going to heal this man; that was probably why he was placed there to begin with. Perhaps Jesus looked at their faces; He searched for any hint of hope and mercy; He probably hoped for the softening of their hearts. He wished they could place themselves in the position of the man with the withered hand. The disabled man sat there knowing in his heart that the Pharisees did not wish him to be healed on that day. He knew that he was being used by the Pharisees as a test against Jesus. He saw the contrast between Jesus' caring expression and that of the hard, cold and emotionless Pharisees. As is normal for a group-oriented society, the

Pharisees would rather have this man suffering, or even sacrificed, than for Jesus to win this battle.

When no mercy was forthcoming from the Pharisees, Jesus displayed defiance: He called the man to the centre of the audience. Jesus wanted everybody to witness the healing and to comprehend the point: People were important to Jesus.

Matt 12:13-14 Then He said to the man, Stretch out your hand. And he stretched it out, and it was restored whole like the other. Then the Pharisees went out and held council against Him, as to how they might destroy Him.

The Pharisees lost this battle against Jesus as indicated by their leaving the synagogue: During public debate the losers always left. They realized that they were not going to end the "Jesus problem" by means of making Jesus destitute of honor. It was a good strategy, however: If they could succeed in causing Jesus to be without honor, no one would have wanted to pay any attention to Him. The only problem with the strategy was that Jesus was much smarter than all of them combined. Every time Jesus won a contest, such as this one, their strategy backfired because they lost honor instead of Jesus. Perhaps that is why a change of course was needed here. Perhaps this is why their strategy against Jesus shifted from questioning Him, attempting to take away His honor, to attempting to trick Him, so that He could be taken to court to try killing Him. The Pharisees left the synagogue to figure out how they might *destroy* Jesus; other strategies were found to be ineffective. Drastic measures were now needed to resolve the "Jesus problem".

Their loss meant triumph for Jesus and the man with the withered hand. Luke told us that the Pharisees were filled with anger; the Greek word being ἄνοια, probably where the English word "annoy" came from. The Pharisees responded by taking the battle to the next level: They agreed to destroy Jesus. This decision confirmed the hardness of their hearts. "To save" society they felt it necessary to sacrifice Jesus.

It was Jesus' selflessness that brought healing to the man with the withered hand. Ironically, it was Jesus' sacrifice, which the Pharisees orchestrated, that made salvation possible, even for the Pharisees. The

Pharisees were actually right: Sacrificing Jesus did bring salvation - not the type of salvation they had in mind, but salvation from sin and death.

❧ CHAPTER TEN ❧

STEREOTYPING AND THE REJECTION OF JESUS

Matt 13:54-57; Mark 6:1-6

As previously indicated, the New Testament people's values were determined by the group to which they belonged. When a society attributed values in this way, group identity became very important. Conformity to the group's identity was also imperative as the group's identity needed to be protected. The result was a group in which all members had the same status, the same ideals and the same mindsets. Non-conformists were turned out from the group to retain conformity; consequently, this system created a haven for stereotyping[71]. When the identity of the group, to which individuals belonged, was identified, people knew a great deal about them: Thus, groups became stereotyped. Stereotyping could be defined as creating an oversimplified or a generalized portrayal of a group. Stereotypes could be accurate or plainly wrong:

- Black people are good dancers
- Chinese people are bad drivers
- Italians are passionate
- Women are emotional, men are insensitive
- Modern day Jews are greedy

---

[71] Esler 2000:328.

- Blond women are dumb
- The French are romantic

Stereotypes were often wrong about people. Yet, all races produced stereotypes about themselves and others. Stereotypes are often wrong in today's society as people are individuals, and individuality is encouraged. Thus, diversity within the group is more variable than generalizations; consequently, it causes such generalizations to be less true. Group identity is no longer defined narrowly. On the other hand, group bonding, loyalty and support are much weaker in today's Western society than that of New Testament groups.

Because conformity was enforced in New Testament society, and as individuals had no value outside of the groups, stereotyping was typically more accurate. People of the same status, in fact, lived in the same neighborhood; and they generally conducted business with people of the same status.[72] People of the same status associated with each other. Association between different status groups, however, did not occur often.

If a person from an honorable group associated with someone from a dishonorable group the honorable person lost honor and the dishonored person gained honor. People with a lower status, therefore, always attempted to associate with people of higher status groups. People of higher status groups always attempted to avoid association with people of lower status groups. There was a tightrope, however, to be walked by those with a lower status: If those people attempted to associate with "higher" people they were rejected by the people with higher status, and such rejection caused the lower persons to fall even lower. In turn, this caused the persons' group to lose honor and, thus moved the group lower down on the status line. This group, however, would then punish the offenders socially. Attempts to associate with higher class people to increase one's own status had to be witnessed clearly to have any value, for society attributed honor or shame; society was the judge.[73] People of higher status never wished to be seen associating with people from below. No wonder that Nicodemus, a ruler, came to Jesus at night. He feared what his group might think of

---

[72] Richards 2008:31.
[73] Neyrey 1998:22.

such a meeting. To protect him from his group the meeting could not be witnessed.

John 3:1-2   And there was a man of the Pharisees named Nicodemus, a ruler of the Jews.   He came to Jesus by night and said to Him, Rabbi, we know that you are a teacher come from God; for no man can do these miracles which you do unless God is with him.

A modern day example of this dynamic at work is where someone knows a person who is respected and honored. During our everyday conversations we tend to mention our association with that esteemed person. The reason why we do this is to elevate our standing. The logic is that if this person is respected and deals with me, I must also have to be esteemed. We call this "name dropping". The New Testament society operated on the same principle, only a very great deal worse. They were always busy working their way up (and down) the status line.

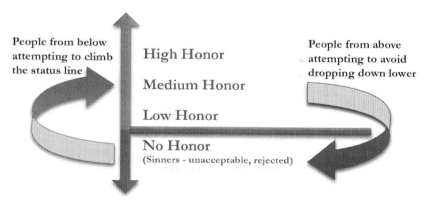

To function in this way, a person had to know the status of another person prior to any dealings between them. There had to be an easy way to know the status of other people. One way of determining status was by associating people with the group to which they belonged. The stereotyping of the group was then superimposed on the relevant person. It was impossible to know the status of every individual, but it was easier to know the status of groups as there were far fewer groups than people. Examples of New Testament group stereotypes were as follows:

- Zealots were violent
- Pharisees, Sadducees, Scribes and Priests were esteemed, righteous, fair and just
- Levites and Benjaminites were esteemed higher than the other tribes
- Sick and disabled people were sinners
- Tax collectors were the lowest of the low

After reading the gospels, it might come as a surprise that Pharisees and Sadducees were esteemed so highly in New Testament times. The gospels stereotyped them unkindly because Jesus exposed their hearts; but the public did not know their hearts and only saw their actions; and action was designed to increase honor.

Matt 23:3-7 Therefore whatever they (Pharisees) tell you to observe, observe and do. But do not do according to their works; for they say, and do not do. For they bind heavy and hard-to-carry burdens and lay them on men's shoulders. But they will not move them with one of their fingers. But they do all their works in order to be seen of men. They make their phylacteries broad and enlarge the borders of their garments. And they love the first couch at feasts, and the chief seats in the synagogues, and greetings in the market-places, and to be called, Rabbi! Rabbi! by men.

The following were examples of how tax collectors were stereotyped:

Mat 5:46 For if you love those who love you, what reward do you have? Do not even the tax-collectors do the same?

Mat 9:11 And when the Pharisees saw, they said to His disciples, Why does your master eat with tax-collectors and sinners?

Mat 21:31 Which of the two did the will of his father? They said to Him, The first. Jesus said to them, Truly I say to you that the tax-collectors and the harlots go into the kingdom of God before you.

It was already demonstrated that the tax collectors were hated by the Zealots; they saw them as traitors. It also needs to be noticed, however, that they were equally despised by the Sadducees. Tax collecting was viewed as being in competition with the much needed temple income.[74] Thus, tax collectors were seen by the Sadducees as working against God.

To be able to ascertain someone's status people were introduced in such a way as to attach them to a specific group; then the person was viewed in the same stereotypical light as the group would be regarded. When a person was introduced as lame, blind, or with a withered hand, the introduction was not only meant to explain the person's predicament, but to tie the person to his or her group, and through the group to the person's status. Such an introduction meant that this person was "grouped" as a sinner and, consequently, with no status and unacceptable.

Being associated with a group meant that people were tied to other people. The person providing the introduction always believed that the audience knew the group to which the announced person was being attached to in the introduction. If the well-known, renowned person's status is acknowledged then the newcomer being associated to that person would have the same status, thanks to stereotyping. This was the real function of genealogies: A person was being tied to others whose status was known. The inference was that the person being introduced shared the status of the people listed in the genealogy.

Jesus was introduced as Jesus, the son of David; James and John were known as the sons of Zebedee. James was introduced as the son of Alpheus, and so the list goes on. People were associated with other people to make known their status level.

Not only were people stereotyped, but places also became stereotyped because of the people who lived there, since people of the same status lived in the same locations. In this way Jerusalem became known as "holy"; Jericho was stereotyped as "rich", and Nazareth as "bad":

John 1:45-46   Philip found Nathanael and said to him, We have found Him of whom Moses wrote in the Law and the Prophets, Jesus

---

[74]   Friedrichsen 2005:108.

of Nazareth, the son of Joseph. And Nathanael said to him, Can there be any good thing come out of Nazareth? Philip said to him, Come and see.

People were often associated with places for the same reason: If a place was stereotyped it was valuable to assess people's status if they were from that location. Jesus was called "Jesus of Nazareth" sixteen times in the gospels alone. Mary was known as "Mary Magdalene"; this probably meant that Mary was from Magdala. Saul was known as "Saul of Tarsus".

To demonstrate how strong these stereotypes were, and to obtain a feeling for the social consequences that resulted from these stereotypes, let us just look at the basis for Jesus' rejection in this story: If Jesus were to live in our individualistic society He would probably have been known as "Jesus the Healer", "Jesus the Preacher", or perhaps as "Jesus, the miracle Man". When we introduce people we introduce them along with their occupation, or something for which they are famous. In the New Testament society individualism was overwritten by the group's status.

Matt 13:54 And when He had come into His own country, He taught them in their synagogue, so much so that they were astonished and said, from where does this man have this wisdom and these mighty works?

The people in the synagogue listened to Jesus as He taught them. Let us note how the audience was astonished: They marveled at Jesus' wisdom and His mighty works. It seemed as if Jesus was highly esteemed here. Let us also note that the basis for Jesus' high honor in this story was an individualistic performance, because of His teaching and works, which was rare. After all, it appeared as though His words and wisdom were more highly esteemed than the regular rabbis who spoke at this synagogue.

In the New Testament Jewish society did not value individualism. The Jews tended strongly towards group orientation. In other words, the group to which Jesus belonged was more powerful in determining His status than His individual accomplishments or words. Now we see by way of one simple statement, why the status of the group to which Jesus belonged, overridden and invalidated the personal status, which He had just earned.

> *Matt 13:55-56 Is not this the carpenter's son? Is not his mother called Mary? And his brothers, James and Joses and Simon and Judas, and his sisters, are they not all with us? Then from where does this man have all these things?*

The question being asked has been, "...we know the group to which Jesus belongs, how could He have risen above them?" The logic has been that Jesus' group has not been that wise, so if Jesus has belonged to this group He could not have been any wiser. Nazareth's status was already low. For the people of Nazareth to look down on Jesus' family had to imply that Jesus' family still had a lower status.

In this type of society it was almost impossible to escape from group's stereotypes. The only way out for the group was to reject a person, or for someone with high honor and authority to attribute honor based on an extraordinary feat, usually associated with the well-being of the group. Consequently, the only regular direction out of a group was down to a lower group, as the attribution of high honor was very rare. Let us notice here how strong the stereotyping is: A few moments ago they marveled at Jesus, and now...

> *Matt 13:57 And they were offended in Him. But Jesus said to them, a prophet is not without honor, except in his own country and in his own house.*

The synagogue-goers were awed and overwhelmed by Jesus, but now they were offended by Him, not for anything He did or said, but simply because of the group He came from. The group's stereotypical classification resulted in Jesus' rejection. It is amazing that Jesus' rejection was not just a mild rejection, but let us notice the strong language: They were "offended"! Stereotypes and group orientation were so strong that neither all the miracles Jesus performed, nor any of His powerful sermons could sway their predetermined views; for these things were regarded as individualistic and individual achievements outside the group were just not valued unless the group benefitted from such individual acts.

A church sign once read: "Some minds are like concrete, thoroughly mixed up and permanently set."[75] Perhaps this was such a case.

---

[75] Brumby, W.Clayton. *The Missing Ministry: Recapturing Church Growth Through Effective Church Sign Evangelism.* San Fransico: Brumby. 1998.

✃ CHAPTER ELEVEN ✄

GOD'S COMMANDMENTS OR HUMAN TRADITION

Matt 15:1-20; Mark 7:1-23

Matt 15:1   Then the scribes and Pharisees who were from Jerusalem came to Jesus, saying...

Jesus was at Gennesaret. To get there from Jerusalem one had to cross over the Sea of Galilee (Matt 14:34). Scribes and Pharisees came to Jesus all the way from Jerusalem; to do so they had to travel a minimum of 68 miles on foot to the nearest edge of the Sea of Galilee, which was the shortest distance. Then they had to rent a boat to cross over to the other side. Considering all the trouble this took, one has to assume that they were on a serious mission. Considering all the effort that went into this journey, one might expect a very serious charge to be brought against Jesus. This assumption is also based upon who these Scribes and Pharisees were: They were not just local Pharisees, but Pharisees from Jerusalem. They were probably the best educated and highly esteemed teachers in the Pharisaic order. Because of the importance and status associated with Jerusalem, especially concerning religious matters, they would have come with the full authority of the religious establishment. Consequently, they would have had a very important reason for this visit. Considering the personal sacrifice involved in making this trip, these men would have been very dedicated to their cause.

Once there it would have been customary for them to introduce themselves and associate themselves with some group or place. This is how Matthew knew where they were from, although that was not the reason for disclosing this information; rather it was to establish the basis of their status. Since their status was much higher than that of Jesus, they continued with their charge. It is interesting to note that they have not been asking whether or not, in actual fact, Jesus transgressed their law. The question automatically assumed guilt and sought an explanation for the transgression.

Matt 15:2 Why do your disciples transgress the tradition of the elders? For they do not wash their hands when they eat bread.

All the effort and exertion to come to where Jesus was just to ask Him this question demonstrated how strongly they felt about "the tradition of the elders": This originally began as an oral tradition with the intent to protect the Mosaic Law by acting as a hedge around it. It was thought that obedience to this tradition would serve as a barrier that would prevent the Jews from breaking the Mosaic Law itself. With time, however, the oral tradition or tradition of the elders became a law unto itself. Hence, Jesus was seen as a law-breaker.

The Mosaic Law, however, did not mandate the ceremonial washing prior to eating. The issue here was not related to "biological" cleanliness. The tradition of the elders referred to by the Pharisees concerned a "ceremonial washing". Since the disciples did not partake in the washing of hands the Pharisees viewed them as spiritually defiled.

The idea of this law originated from the Mosaic Law, stating that priests had to wash in the laver, a Jewish ceremonial basin, before taking the sacrifice into the tent (Exodus 30:17-21). The elders later added that all Jews had to pour water over their hands so as not to make the whole body unclean: The Pharisees referred to the tractate called *Yadayim,* or "hands", here; (cf. Mishnah Yadayim 2:1). Although these "writings" are in written form today, they were still in oral form in Jesus' day. They were literally traditions which grew until they became law. In fact, there is a whole section of the Mishnah and the Tosefta dealing with all the regulations regarding uncleanness of hands and their cleansing. This section is divided into four chapters which contain twenty-two statements in total. The regulations discussed are, amongst others, the following:

> *"Ch. I.: The quantity of water necessary to cleanse the hands by pouring it over them (§ 1); the vessels from which the water may be poured over the hands (§ 2); kinds of water which may not be used to cleanse the hands, and persons who may perform the act of manual ablution (§§ 3-5)."*[76]

> *"Ch. II.: How the water should be poured over the hands, and the first and second ablutions (§§ 1-3); the hands are regarded as clean in all cases where doubt exists as to whether the ablution was properly performed (§ 4)."*[77]

The Jews observed these laws so strictly that the story is told of Rabbi Akiba[78] who was imprisoned, having too little water both to drink and to wash his hands. Instead of drinking the water, he chose rather to wash his hands. He was willing to make this decision even if it might have resulted in his death. It was incomprehensible to the Pharisees that someone would eat without washing his or her hands, thereby violating their law and rendering the body unclean.

The tradition of the elders was, however, *their* law and not God's law. To illustrate the differences between these two sets of laws the following table can serve as an example:

Mosaic Law	Tradition of the Elders
Remember the Sabbath day to keep it Holy. Work should not be done on the Sabbath.	Plucking hands full of grain was determined to be harvesting. Harvesting was seen as

---

[76] "JewishEncyclopedia.com - YADAYIM." JewishEncyclopedia.com. http://www.jewishencyclopedia.com/view.jsp?artid=4&letter=Y (accessed August 24, 2010).

[77] Ibid.

[78] Mindel, Nissan. "Rabbi Akiba in Prison - Rabbi Akiba." Chabad Lubavitch - Torah, Judaism and Jewish Info. http://www.chabad.org/library/article_cdo/aid/111935/jewish/Rabbi-Akiba-in-Prison.htm (accessed August 24, 2010).

(Exodus 20:8-11).	work. Therefore, Jesus and His disciples were working on the Sabbath. (Matthew 12:1-2). A doctor's job was to heal people. A job was viewed as work. Healing on the Sabbath, therefore, was determined to be work. (Matthew 12:10).
Fasting was intended for special occasions, (cf. the book of Esther), or for seeking God's guidance.	Fasting was mandated twice a week. (Luke 18:12).
Priests were to wash in the Laver before entering the tent. (Exodus 30:17-21).	Everyone had to wash hands prior to eating. Failure to wash hands would render the hands unclean, which would in turn render the food unclean, which would render the entire body unclean if consumed. Therefore, a ritual pouring of water over the hands was mandated for all Jews. (Matt 15:2). Please note that in this case it was the unwashed hands which deemed the food unclean, not the actual type of food. Thus, even fruit could become unclean.
Honor your father and your mother. (Exodus 20:12).	Honoring parents included taking care of their financial needs if they could not do so themselves. But people could also declare a "Korban" – dedicating their money to God or for His purposes. Since God is

	more important than people, the Korban overrides the command to sustain parents in need. (Matt 15:4-6).
Swearing in God's name as a promise to do something, forces the person to keep such a promise. (Ex 20:7; Num 30:2).	Many promises were rendered of no consequence unless the promise was made to their specification. (Matt 23:16).

The attack was made: Jesus now had a chance to respond. His response could have been either to defend Himself, or as we have seen Jesus did before, throw back the challenge at them. Jesus actually challenged the very foundation of their attack.

Matt 15:3 But He answered and said to them, why do you also transgress the commandment of God by your tradition?

Surprisingly, Jesus stated that their law stood in violation of God's law. It was almost as if Jesus declared their law unconstitutional. God's law superseded all other laws. Since their law violated God's law, their law was invalid. Once again, Jesus pointed out the cracks in their system. After all, these were traditions of the elders, of men and people in general, rather than laws of God. Since their laws were human laws they lacked any authority by which one could sin against them. It is ironic that they were accusing Jesus of sin for breaching a human tradition, yet *they did not see their own sin in elevating human tradition to the status of the Holy Scriptures.* These laws had to be viewed as "Holy Scriptures" for one to be able to sin against them.

To prove His hypothesis Jesus presented the Pharisees with a few examples of how they argued about God. Jesus demonstrated how their laws contravened the spirit of God's law.

Matt 15:4-6 For God commanded, saying, "Honor your father and mother"; and, "He who speaks evil of father or mother, let him die by death." But you say, whoever says to his father or mother, whatever you would gain from me, it is a gift to God; and in no way he honors

*his father or his mother. And you voided the commandment of God by
your tradition.*

Notice how Jesus contrasted their tradition to God's law. He
referred to what the Scripture said, "God commanded" and to the
tradition of the elders, "you say". Hence, according to Jesus' view God's
words were a great deal more binding than what they said; in fact, Jesus
condemned them.[79] Jesus spoke about the Korban here, which means,
"it is a gift" (cf. tractate Nedarim found in the Mishnah, chapters 1, 9,
and 11).[80] It was common practice in New Testament times and fully
endorsed by the tradition of the elders for people to shirk their
responsibility towards their parents by declaring a "Korban". This
meant that the money was now intended for God's purposes only and
could not be used to sustain their parents, as the law stated. Most of
them, however, found all sorts of creative ways of nullifying such vows
to keep the money. Others simply waited for the demise of their parents
before cancelling their Korban vows.

The "tradition of the elders" knew what the intent of God's law
was, but found technical ways to maneuver around God's laws, and
transgressed the letter of God's law with some "creative logic". The
intent of God's law, however, was clearly desecrated. Jesus called such
maneuvering around God's law, the "voiding of the commandment of
God". Jesus now went to the heart of the issue at hand:

*Matt 15:7-9 Hypocrites! Well did Isaiah prophesy of you, saying,
"This people draws near to Me with their mouth, and honors Me with
their lips, but their heart is far from Me. But in vain they worship
Me, teaching for doctrines the commandments of men."*

Jesus quoted Isaiah 29:13. There was not a better description of
the Pharisees' problem than this. They pretended to be "godly" in their
speech and designed their actions to demonstrate their "godliness"
outwardly, but it was only pretense, as their hearts were far from God.

---

[79] Driggers 2007:236.
[80] "Wikisource - Mishnah/Seder Nashim/Tractate Nedarim" Wikisource.org.
http://en.wikisource.org/wiki/Mishnah/Seder_Nashim/Tractate_Nedarim
(accessed August 24, 2010).

Their worship of God was not genuine worship to begin with: It was a show to gain human honor and admiration. They taught their own corrupt ways as laws around God's laws. In many ways the tradition of the elders was designed to escape from the very demands of God's law, although that was not the original intent of the oral tradition.

This story did not address, as some suppose, the topic of clean and unclean types of foods. It addressed the Pharisaic view that non-adherence to certain rules and human tradition could make any type of food unclean, which then would defile a person. This topic was clarified by Jesus. Let us please note how He disagreed with the Pharisaic view:

Matt 15:20 ... But eating with unwashed hands does not make anyone unclean.

Pierre F. Steenberg, Ph.D., D.Min.

❧ CHAPTER TWELVE ❧

VYING FOR POSITION

Matt 18:1-5; 20:20-24; Mark 9:33-37; 10:35-45; Luke 9:46-48

The disciples often heard Jesus preaching. One topic that seemed central to Jesus' preaching was the "kingdom". The kingdom was compared to many things such as a treasure, leaven and a mustard seed. The disciples heard from these comparisons that the kingdom would grow and spread. They also heard that admission to this kingdom was more highly prized than anything else, including all our possessions. Admission to this kingdom of God was of the utmost importance. Examples and references are:

Kingdom Comparison	Reference	Message
Mustard seed	Matt 13:31	The kingdom will grow
Leaven	Matt 13:33	The kingdom will spread
Hidden treasure	Matt 13:44	The kingdom is worth more than anything else
A merchant seeking beautiful pearls	Matt 13:45	The kingdom is worth more than anything else
Like a net being cast out	Matt 13:47	Some make it into the kingdom, others do not

Like a king who holds a marriage feast	Matt 22:2	Not all are worthy of the kingdom

It was also heard from Jesus that the kingdom was at hand. The expectation of the kingdom was not seen as something that would come in the distant future, but in their lifetime.

Matt 4:17 From that time Jesus began to preach and to say, Repent! For the kingdom of Heaven is at hand.

It is worth noting here that the kingdom Jesus refers to does not point to heaven, unless the text actually says, "the kingdom of heaven". The term "kingdom" when it appears alone, especially in the book of Matthew, refers to God's kingship, rule or reign in the hearts of people, particularly after the resurrection when the Christian church began. Sometimes Jesus spoke of the earthly kingdom and sometimes He spoke of the heavenly kingdom. Confusion between these two concepts of kingdom can easily occur. What Jesus said about the one was often taken as referring to the other. Remember how the Jews charged Jesus politically in front of Pilate…and let us listen to the exchange between the two of them on the topic of the kingdom:

John 18:36-37 Jesus replied, 'Mine is not a kingdom of this world; if my kingdom were of this world, my men would have fought to prevent my being surrendered to the Jews. As it is, my kingdom does not belong here.' Pilate said, 'So, then you are a king?' Jesus answered, 'It is you who say that I am a king. I was born for this, I came into the world for this, to bear witness to the truth; and all who are on the side of truth listen to my voice.'

Pilate saw Jesus' kingdom in the context of an earthly kingdom as one would expect him to do since he functioned in that milieu. To Pilate, a Roman, the political world view overshadowed the religious world view. Thus, it is only natural for Pilate to think first of an earthly political kingdom. This time, however, Jesus talked about the kingdom in the context of the heavenly kingdom. At other times Jesus spoke about an earthly kingdom; for example, let us notice how Jesus stated that this kingdom referred to God's will being done on earth; rule...

Matt 6:10 Your kingdom come, Your will be done, on earth as it is in Heaven.

In Jesus' teaching here in Matthew 6 about prayer He also instructed His disciples to pray for the kingdom to come. In fact, Jesus refers to the kingdom twice in the short prayer; once in verse ten above and once in verse thirteen:

Matt 6:13 And lead us not into temptation, but deliver us from the evil. For Yours is the kingdom, and the power, and the glory, forever. Amen.

Jesus also linked admission to the kingdom to a relationship with Him. Any person who confessed Jesus would be acknowledged by the Father. Any person who believed Jesus would not be condemned.

Matt 10:32 Then everyone who shall confess Me before men, I will confess him before My Father who is in Heaven.

John 3:18 He who believes on Him is not condemned, but he who does not believe is condemned already, because he has not believed in the name of the only-begotten Son of God.

John 6:40 And this is the will of Him who sent Me, that everyone who sees the Son and believes on Him should have everlasting life. And I will raise him up at the last day.

One has to ask, what were the disciples thinking when they heard all these messages from Jesus? Their own context consisted of a society divided into many status groups. It would be normal for them to think that Jesus was in the process of creating a new group referred to as a part of the kingdom. Since Jesus used a royal term, king, to refer to this group they would have assumed that the "new group" would enjoy the highest honor. After all, if God's will would take place in this new group, that group would be blessed. Being blessed by God in religion meant to be blessed with many sons, that is to say kinship, with riches, namely the economy, and with honor and power, i.e. politics.

The disciples transplanted their world view of how things worked in their society in the way they assumed it would be going to work in the kingdom. They projected their situation and understanding onto the kingdom. By doing so they assumed many things about the kingdom. Combining their own context with what they heard about the kingdom the disciples began to construct a framework of thinking about the kingdom. Based on what is known about what Jesus said and how their context worked they might have assumed the following:

1. The kingdom was coming: Jesus said so.
2. People got into the kingdom through Jesus: Jesus said so.
3. There were different classes of people in society, therefore, there would be different classes of people in the kingdom: The disciple's assumption based on Matt 5:19.
4. There were rich and poor people in society, therefore, there would be rich and poor people in the kingdom: The disciples' assumption.
5. Society was governed, therefore, the kingdom would also be governed: The disciples' assumption.
6. The elite ruled over the rest of the populace, therefore, there would be ruling elite in the kingdom: The disciples' assumption.
7. The disciples were Jesus' special friends, therefore, they would be getting into the kingdom and would also be special and honored there: The disciples' assumption.

We might be excused for thinking that these assumptions were presumptuous and wrong. When we think this way, however, we make the same mistake as the disciples have made because we also have a context, although a different one, that we now superimpose on the situation, and that in turn determines our interpretation. We have to remember that we also read the disciple's words, written down after "the penny dropped" and after their understanding had changed. Nevertheless, given their context, how their society and world views functioned, it was easy to see how they could have thought when they reasoned this way when they had heard Jesus speaking at that stage before the cross; rather than understanding their thinking about the same assumptions after the cross and resurrection when these events gained new meaning. There was indeed some basis for their assumptions, for Jesus said:

> *Matt 5:19 Therefore whoever shall relax one of these commandments, the least, and shall teach men so, he shall be called the least in the kingdom of Heaven. But whoever shall do and teach them, the same shall be called great in the kingdom of Heaven.*

Heard by someone who lived in a society shaped by honor and shame where people were grouped according to their social status, it might have sounded as if Jesus said that there would be different classes of people, those called "the least" and those called "great", in the kingdom of heaven. It also might have been assumed with Jesus' prayer about, "on earth as it is in Heaven", that it would also apply to the earthly kingdom. Based on Jesus' words, they assumed and saw a picture of the kingdom which looked just like their New Testament society:

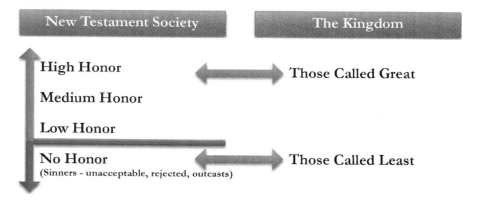

A person's father was one source of status, honor or shame, in the New Testament society. God was the King in the kingdom. Jesus taught His disciples to pray, "our Father", making the King also their Father. If they were the King's sons, they would have the King's honor. Consequently, in the kingdom, they were to be honored. The difference then between the New Testament society and the kingdom is that different people would be honored or shamed in the kingdom than in their current groups. There would be a trading of places, as it were: In their New Testament society they did not have much honor; Matthew was a tax-collector, but in the kingdom they were going to enjoy great honor. Those who had high honor in their society were going to be moved down the status line to lower honor, as they were not Jesus' special friends and as they did not belong to Jesus' group.

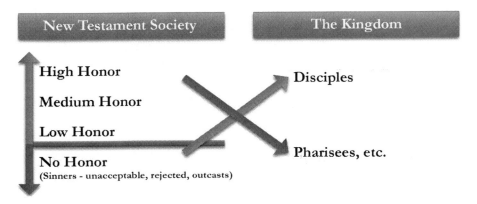

In Luke's gospel, Luke 11, and in the latter part of Matthew's gospel, Matthew 23, the disciples heard Jesus conveying numerous statements to the Pharisees. These pronouncements were by no means flattering. In fact, these statements began with an exclamation of grief and anguish, "woe to you". When the disciples heard Jesus calling the Pharisees hypocrites, blind, whitewashed tombs and serpents they could not misunderstood these words as if they honored them. Jesus declared that they had no honor, they were shameful. There was no honor in their behavior since they were hypocrites and there was no honor in their health for they were disabled, blind, and, therefore, were considered by Jesus to be sinners. The logical conclusion the disciples reached was that they did not have much honor in their society while the Pharisees had high honor, but according to Jesus' assessment the disciples were going to be honored while the Pharisees would be shamed in the kingdom.

A second source of status in the New Testament society was behavior. Certain behavior was deemed honorable and other behavior shameful. What one did, resulted in society's bestowal of honor or shame. With this mindset the disciples heard Jesus saying:

Matt 16:27 For the Son of Man shall come in the glory of His Father with His angels, and then He shall reward each one according to his works.

The disciples might have taken this statement to mean that the Father would reward people, based on their behavior. In other words, according to the New Testament Jewish mindset, the Father bestowed honor or shame on people based on whether they behaved in a certain way or avoided other behavior. They might have reasoned that this was proof that there would be different classes of people in the kingdom as behavior differ from person to person, therefore, honor and shame would differ from person to person, resulting in different status classes.

After hearing such statements from Jesus it was only natural that they would have expected great honor in the kingdom:

- Firstly, the King is their Father; honor by birth and kinship.
- Secondly, they had a privileged position with Jesus; honor by association.
- Thirdly, they had given up everything to follow Him; honor by sacrifice.
- Lastly, they thought their works were just fabulous; honor by behavior.

It would have been normal for them to start thinking about their roles in the kingdom. Maybe they also started dreaming about the abundance of honor being bestowed on them in the kingdom, for Jesus said:

John 12:26 If anyone serves Me, let him follow Me; and where I am, there also My servant shall be. If anyone serves Me, the Father will honor him.

Matt 5:12 Rejoice and be exceedingly glad, for your reward in Heaven is great. For so they persecuted the prophets who were before you.

No one else served Jesus as they did; therefore, they thought no one else would have as much honor as that they were going to receive. Even if their following Jesus would result in dishonor, persecution now, they would be rewarded in the kingdom. Their thoughts developed into expectations. When Jesus told the rich man that he was to sell all his belongings, the disciples were perplexed:

Matt 19:25-26 When His disciples heard, they were exceedingly amazed, saying, Who then can be saved? But Jesus looked on them and said to them, with men this is impossible, but with God all things are possible.

They were amazed at Jesus' argument because that contradicted their world view. They believed that the rich were rich because of God's blessings: Religious success resulted in economic success. Yet, to enter the kingdom people needed to let go of their God-given blessings, riches. No wonder they asked who could be saved as no riches meant on no account religious success, and no religious success left people lost. Subsequently, Peter's mind kicked into high gear: His question demonstrated their expectations to be honored. If the rich man would be saved once he sold off his riches, and the disciples already had given up all they had, they would be saved; if this was the case, they could have merely taken their salvation for granted. With that worry out of the way, Peter was concerned about the next topic, his expected reward:

Matt 19:27 Then answering Peter said to Him, Behold, we have forsaken all and have followed You. Therefore what shall we have?

Coming from the typical New Testament Jewish mindset it would seem as if Jesus confirmed Peter's expectation: They would be honored. Their honor would come in the form of a high position; they would be elevated above all the others:

Matt 19:28 And Jesus said to them, Truly I say to you that you who have followed Me, in the regeneration, when the Son of Man shall sit in the throne of His glory, you also shall sit on twelve thrones, judging the twelve tribes of Israel.

Based upon everything they thought they knew of the kingdom so far, they now began to vie for a position: All positions have ranks, and some positions were more important, with more status, than others. Positions with a high status were always fewer in supply than those with little honor. If high positions were limited, as they always were, then they found themselves in competition for those positions; therefore, they had to vie for positions. Vying for positions also confirmed what they were thinking about. In general, thought processes came before arguments, and arguments usually did not start before this specific thinking process festered in the mind for some time.

Mark 9:33-34 And He came to Capernaum. And being in the house, He asked them, what was it that you disputed among yourselves in the way? But they were silent. For in the way they had disputed among themselves who was the greatest.

Luke 9:46 And an argument came in among them, who might be the greater of them.

It was also known that the disciples had thought about these matters as they once asked this very question in a veiled manner. They were trying to find out what Jesus thought about them, specifically who was the greatest. They asked the question without directly referring directly to their own wishes. They hoped that Jesus would have provided at least a hint.

Matt 18:1 At that hour the disciples came to Jesus, saying, Who is the greater in the kingdom of Heaven?

There was one sure way to settle these arguments: Have the person with the right to confer honor, confer it? James and John came to Jesus with this intention. They wished to settle this matter by claiming their prime positions of honor:

Mark 10:35-37 And James and John, the sons of Zebedee, came up to Him, saying, Master, we desire that You should do for us whatever we shall ask. And He said to them, what do you desire that I should do for you? They said to Him, Grant to us that we may sit, one on Your right hand and the other on Your left hand, in Your glory.

"Table seating" positions in New Testament times were determined by those with the highest honor.[81] The most honorable person sat at the head of the table. The second most important person sat on the right side of the most important person. The third most important person sat on the left side. This sequence then would continue all the way down and around the table. By requesting the right and left seats James and John requested the highest two positions of honor. They placed themselves on top of the status line in the kingdom, just below Jesus. This also meant that the other disciples were pushed down the table and thus, down the status line. No wonder the other disciples did not like what they heard:

Mark 10:41 And when the ten heard, they began to be indignant with James and John.

Arranging people according to status when seated at a table in New Testament times also appeared in one of Jesus' parables. In fact, this teaching on honor and shame did not just appear here, it seemed to be the central theme as no other information, for example, who was getting married, was given about the event.[82] This New Testament story taught us about the rules of seating and how honor and shame determined positions:

Luke 14:7-10 And He put forth a parable to those who were invited, when He noted how they chose out the chief places, saying to them, when you are invited by anyone to a wedding, do not recline in the chief seat, lest a more honorable man than you may be invited by him. And he who invited you and him shall come and say to you, give place to this man; and then you begin with shame to take the last place. But when you are invited, go and recline in the lowest place, so that when he who invited you comes, he may say to you, Friend, go up higher. Then glory shall be to you before those reclining with you.

---

[81] Downing 1999:53.
[82] Downing 1999:53.

Plutarch also displayed wisdom with regard to this matter of honor and shame at meal tables and using seating positions as a measuring stick of honor or shame. He wrote:

"When we have taken our places we ought not to try to discover who has been placed above us, but rather how we may be thoroughly agreeable to those placed with us, by trying at once to discover in them something that may serve to initiate and maintain friendship, for, in every case, a man who objects to his place at table is objecting to his neighbor rather than his host, and makes himself objectionable to both." (Moralia 2)

Jesus taught several times on this topic. Every time his message was the same. He either told His disciples not to seek the honorable seats, or He demonstrated how the Pharisees and hypocrites sought honor.

Matt 23:6 And they love the first couch at feasts, and the chief seats in the synagogues.

Mark 12:38-39 And He said to them in His teaching, Beware of the scribes, who love to walk about in robes, and love greetings in the markets, and the chief seats in the synagogues, and the uppermost places at feasts.

James and John wished to have it all. They were claiming the very thing Jesus accused the Pharisees of. In their defense it would be said that honor was sought after more than riches. Honor resulted in riches anyway, but dishonorable riches, for example prostitution, lead to social rejection and shame. They were "sons of thunder"; they were not going to give up:

Matt 20:20-21 Then the mother of Zebedee's children came to Him with her sons, worshiping and desiring a certain thing from Him. And He said to her, what do you desire? She said to Him, grant that these my two sons may sit in Your kingdom, the one on Your right hand and the other on the left.

It is interesting how much their mother also wished them to have it all. She wanted very badly for her sons to be honored. She came to Jesus literally begging; as the text said she came worshipping him. When we worship Jesus because of who He is, it is one thing, but when we worship Jesus because we want something, that is another matter altogether. The Greek word used for worship here means to kiss someone like a dog licking a hand. She was not really worshipping Him, she was soft soaping Him, trying with flattery to persuade Him; her desire for her sons to be honored was extremely strong.

It was no wonder, as a consequence, that Jesus has "instituted" the washing of feet while teaching the disciples about serving rather than being served, for in God's kingdom the one who would be least, would be first.

❧ CHAPTER THIRTEEN ❧

THE WEDDING AT CANA

John 2:1-11

Even a cursory reading of the New Testament makes it abundantly clear that Jesus performed thousands of miracles. He even may have healed millions of people. It is astounding that He went from village to village and healed *everybody*. Jesus may have not proved very popular with physicians as they found themselves without any patients after Jesus had left. No one remained sick after meeting Jesus.

> *Matt 9:35 And Jesus went about all the cities and villages, teaching in their synagogues, and preaching the gospel of the kingdom, and healing every sickness and every disease among the people.*

Jesus performed so many miracles that John gave up recording them. He merely stated that Jesus had done a great deal more than what he wrote down.

> *John 20:30 And truly Jesus did many other signs in the presence of His disciples, which are not written in this book.*

In fact, John did not believe it to be possible to record everything Jesus did. This is a remarkable statement from John considering that Jesus' ministry only lasted three and a half years. After all, how much can a person achieve in such a short time?

John 21:25   And there are also many things, whatever Jesus did, which, if they should be written singly, I suppose the world itself could not contain the books that would be written. Amen.

According to John Jesus performed these miracles in the presence of the disciples. They witnessed these events. They witnessed so many miracles that they could not write them all down. Consequently, they had access to thousands of miracles, stored in their memories. With access to so many stories, yet, choosing to record only a few, one has to come to the conclusion that they had handpicked which stories to use for a particular reason. There must be a reason why someone would chose to record story A, but not stories B, C and D. There would be something in story A that the writer wished to share, warranting the story's choice.

The story of Jesus turning water into wine[83] was a story where its purpose has troubled many people. Why did John include this story in his gospel? What is its message? What was John attempting to teach

---

[83]   There has been a lot of debate whether Jesus provided grape juice or alcoholic wine here. This debate falls outside the scope of this book. A few arguments, however, would be presented briefly with regard to this issue. Since the image of drinking from the cup is used both here and in the "communion" texts, the similarities between the texts can be used to reach some conclusions on this topic. At communion the bread symbolized Jesus' body and it had to be unleavened bread. Leaven seems to represent sin. Unleavened bread, therefore, symbolized Jesus' sinlessness. In the same way the "wine" represented Jesus' blood. It makes no sense at all that the bread had to be unleavened while the "wine" could have been fermented, containing leaven or yeast. Both the bread and the "wine" had to be pure from leaven or yeast, fermentation, to represent Jesus. The "wine" used at communion was grape juice; nothing containing leaven or yeast was allowed in the Jewish home during Passover. Hence, the wine in John's story was also grape juice since here too it represented Jesus' blood. Secondly, the Bible clearly classifies drunkenness as sin (1 Cor. 6:10; Gal 5:21). Since Jesus knew that wedding feasts lasted several days, with people drinking throughout the feast, He knew that drunkenness was inevitable if the "wine" contained alcohol. Would Jesus supply something that He knew would result in sin? Lastly then, the text itself tells us that Jesus' "wine" was different and better from the wine which ran out. The Greek word for "wine" was used interchangeably for both alcoholic wine and grape juice in the New Testament.

his readers? Why was emphasis placed on this story by making it the first recorded miracle in the book of John? The miracle seemed rather insignificant compared to the other miracles where Jesus healed people, saved their lives, drove out demons and demonstrated His power over nature by calming the sea. Is this miracle really included in the Bible just because it showed Jesus saving someone's self-esteem, because he ran out of wine during a wedding celebration? Surely, there has to be more to this story.

Drawing attention to a Jewish wedding with all its customs and symbolism might well have formed the basis of understanding a great deal of the imagery Jesus and many other New Testament authors used. Understanding the Jewish wedding customs and symbolism unlocks the secrets of many passages which makes no sense to us without this understanding. Perhaps John was laying the groundwork to assist us making sense of these passages.

In New Testament times a man, wising to get married to someone's daughter, first had to discuss the matter with the potential father-in-law. This could also have been done by the groom's father or by a "matchmaker;" a broker of marriages. Paul describes himself as a matchmaker between Jesus, the Groom and the believers, the bride.

2 Cor 11:2 For I am jealous over you with godly jealousy. For I have espoused you to one Man, to present you as a pure virgin to Christ.

This conversation between the bride's father and the groom would revolve around the status level of both families[84]. The father would not allow the marriage of his daughter to a man from a lower standing[85]. Marriages bonded the two families together and thus fused their status[86]. Typically the groom and the bride would come from similar status groups. If one of them came from a higher status than the other, the person with the higher status' group would lose status and the lower person's group would gain status. Lower status people would be amendable to such an agreement, but higher people would not be.

---

[84] Arranging a marriage was seen as an honor or shame interaction. An imbalance of status could have prevented New Testament marriages. Hellerman 2000:219.
[85] Chance 1994:140-141.
[86] May 1997:203.

The second point of discussion would be the dowry or price paid for the bride. The bride's father would portray her as a jewel in order to increase the dowry. He would also puff up the family and their status. Jesus, who is often described as a Groom in the New Testament, also paid a dowry for His bride, the believers. Unlike other grooms who typically attempted to negotiate the price down, Jesus paid the highest price possible - His own life. Thus, the New Testament teaches that Christians were bought for a price…

1 Cor 7:23 You are bought with a price, do not be the slaves of men.

Once an agreement about the bride's price was reached the groom had to make his intentions known to the future bride. It was commonly believed that when a man and a woman were alone in private intimate incidents *would* happen. As a result, privacy prior to the actual wedding was never allowed. The groom had to make his intentions known to her in front of other people. This often took place in the form of a meal between the two families. If the groom's intentions were met with enthusiasm by the bride he would pass her a cup of wine. This gesture represented the actual modern question: "Would you marry me?" Her acceptance of the wine, demonstrated by drinking of the cup was viewed as her acceptance of the proposal and would signal a permanent commitment to their relationship.

Notice how Jesus made His covenant contract known to us in the form of a meal and how He gave us the cup of wine, thereby requesting acceptance of the proposal. The proposal even hinted how much the dowry would be: Nothing less than the pouring out of His life blood.

Luke 22:20 In the same way He took the cup, after having dined, saying, this cup is the new covenant in My blood, which is being poured out for you.

To drink of the cup with someone after it had already been accepted by another person indicated a new proposal and, thus, it was assumed that the current betrothal was due to unfaithfulness. Jesus gave the assurance that this would never happen, that He was faithful to His bride, the church. Jesus was tested severely on paying the dowry: He had to sacrifice His life. If He did not persist with the dowry the marriage would have been off. Just like He invited people to "marry" Him by giving them the cup to drink, so His Father invited Him to pay the dowry by sacrificing His life for us by using the marriage imagery of the drinking of the cup.

> *Matt 26:42 He went away again the second time and prayed, saying, My Father, if this cup may not pass away from Me unless I drink it, Your will be done.*

The "cup" referred to the marriage customs of the time. It symbolized sharing of good and bad, sharing everything life has to offer and also suffering. Drinking the cup meant partaking wholly in the other person's life, fulfilling the conditions of the proposal's promises including the payment of the dowry, faithfulness, etc. Jesus referred to His paying the dowry as drinking from the cup.

> *John 18:11 Then Jesus said to Peter, Put up your sword into the sheath. The cup which My Father has given Me, shall I not drink it?*

Now the words of Jesus to James and John about sharing His cup made more sense. Jesus was asking them if they were willing to share His life of suffering with Him, just as in "marriage". Jesus was saying, "if you want to marry (spiritually) Me, you will have to share My life and My life is a life of suffering."

> *Mark 10:37-39 They said to Him, Grant to us that we may sit, one on Your right hand and the other on Your left hand, in Your glory. But Jesus said to them, You do not know what you ask. Can you drink of the cup that I drink of, and be baptized with the baptism that I am baptized with? And they said to Him, We can. And Jesus said to them, You shall indeed drink of the cup that I drink of, and with the baptism that I am baptized with you shall be baptized.*

Now it also made sense what Jesus meant when He said:

1 Cor 10:21 You cannot drink the cup of the Lord and the cup of demons; you cannot be partakers of the Lord's table and of a table of demons.

Jesus stated that one had to make a choice of whose cup one wished to drink from. A person could not be betrothed to two grooms at the same time. One could not celebrate the consummated weddings at the wedding tables of two different grooms. A choice had to be made! Jesus wanted people to accept the cup of invitation. He was preparing the bride's mansion. He would come to claim believers as His bride and would take them to His Father's house and would cover them with His love.

Song 2:4 He brought me to the banqueting house, and His banner over me was love.

Once the cup has been accepted and drunk they were betrothed. Betrothal was much stronger than today's engagements. It could not be broken and the only way out was through divorce. The young women could also reject the proposal by not taking the wine, resulting in an end to the relationship. This is why Joseph needed to divorce Mary if he wanted out, even though they were not married yet.

Matt 1:19 But Joseph, her husband to be, being just, and not willing to make her a public example, he purposed to put her away secretly.

In order to seal the betrothal she had to drink the wine and he had to pay the dowry. They would remain separate until the actual wedding. During the time of separation he would prepare their living quarters, typically a room in his father's home. The father would determine when the room was satisfactorily prepared. Arrangements were also made for the time of the wedding feast. Since the intention of marriage also involved procreation, and included the idea of expanding the family, this task was more complex than just cleaning out the groom's room inside the father's house. In most cases it involved building new quarters onto, or next to, the father's house. This would require more time than just a week or two. Similarly, she would use this time to prepare her wedding garments. There was no set length of time for the preparation phase. Notice how Jesus also goes to prepare a room for His bride and how He promised to come back to claim His bride to be together forever. Notice also that the room is in His Father's house, just like the New Testament model.

> *John 14:2-3 In My Father's house are many mansions; if it were not so, I would have told you. I go to prepare a place for you. And if I go and prepare a place for you, I will come again and receive you to Myself, so that where I am, you may be also.*

Many Bible students have wondered what Jesus meant when He said:

> *Matt 24:36 But of that day and hour no one knows, no, not the angels of Heaven, but only My Father.*

Seen in the light of New Testament wedding imagery it makes perfect sense. Jesus as the Son did not know when the wedding feast would take place because it was up to the Father to determine when the room was suitably prepared. It was up to the Father to decide when there has been adequate preparation for the celebration feast. Since these were the Father's decisions only He knew the outcome of these decisions.

When the father made his decision and declared everything ready the groom would make his way to the bride's home to claim her as his wife. The entire wedding party would accompany him on this trip. Since lighting a torch was part of the tradition, this trip usually happened at night. Loud shouts were given to announce their arrival. She had to be ready.

> *Matt 25:1-6 Then shall the kingdom of Heaven be likened to ten virgins, who took their lamps and went out to meet the bridegroom. And five of them were wise, and five were foolish. The foolish ones took their lamps, but took no oil with them. But the wise took oil in their vessels with their lamps. While the bridegroom tarried, they all slumbered and slept. And at midnight there was a cry made, Behold, the bridegroom comes! Go out to meet him.*

After the bride was received the wedding party usually returned to the groom's father's home. Here the wedding feast would be waiting. It was an opportunity to demonstrate the family's honor and status. If this family was not found to own the honor and status as previously thought, there might have been severe social consequences enforced onto the family. They could lose their entire honor and may even be rejected totally. The feast was not a time to suffer embarrassment.

The groom and bride would then spend time privately to consummate their marriage. She had to be found pure or the deal was off and her family shamed. The groom would speak out after the consummation to signal the completion of the marriage. The best man who waited outside to hear the groom's voice would then make the announcement to the wedding guests.

John 3:29 He who has the bride is the bridegroom, but the friend of the bridegroom who stands and hears him rejoices greatly because of the bridegroom's voice. Then my joy is fulfilled.

Here John the Baptist saw himself as Jesus' best man, preaching to announce the arrival of Jesus the Groom. The first coming of the groom was to broker the betrothal, to invite the bride to share the cup and to pay the dowry. Now, believers yet again awaited the Groom's arrival, this time for the wedding feast. Jesus left believers with the promise that He would remain faithful until united with them in His Father's kingdom; then the feast would begin. Remember, drinking of the cup with someone else constituted a new marriage proposal. Here, Jesus pledged that He would be faithful by not drinking of the cup until the wedding feast.

Matt 26:29 But I say to you, I will not drink of this fruit of the vine from now on, until that day when I drink it new with you in My Father's kingdom.

Just like the groom's wedding party arrived at the bride's home with shouts to announce their arrival and to claim the bride, Jesus would come from His Father's house with shouts and trumpets to announce His coming.

Matt 24:31 And He shall send His angels with a great sound of a trumpet, and they shall gather His elect from the four winds, from one end of the heavens to the other.

1 Thes 4:16 For the Lord Himself shall descend from Heaven with a shout, with the voice of the archangel and with the trumpet of God. And the dead in Christ shall rise first.

The book of Revelation spoke of this wedding feast as an experience of gladness, joy and glory. What a wonderful day that would be!

Rev 19:7 Let us be glad and rejoice and we will give glory to Him. For the marriage of the Lamb has come, and His wife has prepared herself.

At this feast it was customary for the bride and groom, for the second time, to drink a cup of wine together. They would be met with shouts of *"mazel tov"* – congratulations. It was probably with this imagery in mind that Jesus said He would not drink of the cup until He drank it anew with His bride in the kingdom.

John's story of Jesus turning water into wine shed light on many New Testament stories. In fact it laid the very foundation of Jesus' mission and salvation. This story is really a great deal more than a simple miracle. *The wedding imagery employed here served as a summary of the entire salvation story.*

Mary, Jesus' mother attended the wedding with Jesus and His disciples. Everything would have gone well until it happened:

John 2:1-3 And the third day there was a marriage in Cana of Galilee. And the mother of Jesus was there. And Jesus and His disciples were both invited to the marriage. And when they lacked wine, the mother of Jesus said to Him, they have no wine.

Even in today's society this would have been rather embarrassing. In New Testament times embarrassment was linked to shame. The society used shame to embarrass and reject people. Similarly, embarrassment led to shame. Whenever someone was embarrassed it was automatically shameful. Shame also meant the loss of honor. When a person lost honor the entire group, to whom the person belonged to, also lost a portion of their honor. It does not require a vivid imagination to envisage how the members of the group would have reacted to losing their honor due to what some member of the group did or did not do.

This family in all probability puffed up their status in the negotiation process with the bride's father to persuade him that they were of similar or higher status as he was. Now, they ran out of wine! The guests would no doubt have questioned this family's honor. If the family in question were found to have lower honor than promised before, the entire wedding could have been at risk. The master of the feast, probably a prominent slave, who became head slave, would also have been surprised. Had the groom not planned properly? Surely, the shortage was due to negligence. These wedding celebrations lasted for several days. As Jesus and the disciples were invited to the wedding it seems reasonable to assume that Jesus would not get to the wedding on the last day. The invitation suggests that Jesus went to the wedding deliberately rather than just attending the wedding by accident. Jesus' arrival must have been towards the beginning of the celebration rather than towards the end. It was understandable that the wine could have run out on the last day or even perhaps on the second to last day. It seemed, however, as though the wine ran out rather quickly. In other words, this was not just an accident; this was gross underestimation and a lack of planning the needed amount of wine. Yet, preparations for the ceremonial washing indicated no underestimation at all.

John 2:6 And there were six stone water pots there, according to the purification of the Jews, each containing two or three measures.

The fact that *six* water pots were available for ceremonial washing prior to eating demonstrated that many guest were expected. There seems to be a large disparity here between the amounts of wine *vis-à-vis* the amounts of water being made available. Each of these pots could hold about twenty to thirty gallons. One-hundred and twenty to one-hundred and eighty gallons of water was a lot of water for people to just dip their fingers into. Make no mistake, they were expecting many guests. It was surprising that their purification water was so well organized, yet the wine ran out so quickly. Since the topic of ceremonial washing had been discussed before, this topic would not be dwelt upon here. It also demonstrated that this was a proper New Testament Jewish wedding because the hosts were complying with the Pharisaic laws. Perhaps some of the guests were Pharisees themselves. Jesus' solution was to turn the water into wine: Into the best wine.

So why did Jesus use these six jars for the wine? Why did He not just have the empty wine sacks refilled? The issue about not placing new wine into old sacks lest they would tear did not apply here as the wine was to be consumed right away. Fermentation which caused the expansion of the wine would tear the wine sacks, was not about to cause any damage for the next few days of the feast. Why then, use the six jars? Was Jesus making an important statement?

Remember how the priests had to wash their hands at the laver before going into the tent, and how New Testament Jews believed that the human body was the temple of God. They believed, therefore, that nothing could go into the body without washing their hands. Washing represented purification. There was, however, one major difference between the laver washing in the Old Testament on the one hand, and the New Testament society's teaching, on the other hand. In the Old Testament the washing took place after the blood sacrifice. The teaching of the New Testament society dealt with the same cleansing and purification, but without any blood sacrifice. Consequently, Old Testament people were taught that salvation was as a result of sacrifice and after the sacrifice came cleansing. The New Testament's society developed a false belief that they could just cleanse and purify themselves without the blood sacrifice. These six stone jars were the symbol of salvation by works; salvation without the substitutive sacrifice. They believed in essence that they could purify themselves by using a ritual rather than by the sacrifice of blood, which also symbolized Jesus' sacrifice on the cross.

What Jesus did here was very special. He totally removed the ability and means by which they purified themselves. In the water's place Jesus supplied wine, the very symbol of his blood. Jesus was preaching a loud and clear message here through this act. This message was profoundly striking. Jesus was saying, "I am removing the water by which you cleanse and purify yourselves and in its place I am supplying my blood by which you are truly washed and saved."

John 2:9-10 When the ruler of the feast had tasted the water which was made wine (and did not know where it was from, but the servants who drew the water knew), the master of the feast called the bridegroom. And he said to him, every man at the beginning sets forth good wine, and when men have drunk well, then that which is worse. You have kept the good wine until now.

Indeed, Jesus' wine was sweeter and better than any other. His salvation was sweet and satisfying indeed. He saved them with his blood, but he also saved the groom's family from disgrace. It was interesting that the ruler's honor was not at stake, but that of the groom's family. The ruler called the bridegroom and questioned how he prepared the wine. It would seem as if it was the groom's call and, therefore, it would have had an impact on his honor.

Jesus did care about this man's embarrassment. Jesus always cares about our problems even when they might not be life threatening. Jesus was truly compassionate. This, however, was not the only reason why John told this story. Perhaps he wished to set the stage for understanding so many other topics such as the deeper theological implications of the last supper, communion, the second coming, acceptance of salvation, and so forth. Most of all, however, John wanted us to know that we cannot purify ourselves but by the blood of the Lamb. New Testament stories come alive when the culture, habits, symbolism and imagery of New Testament living is understood.

❦ CHAPTER FOURTEEN ❧

THE TEN LEPERS

Luke 17:11-19

Luke 17:11-19 And as He went to Jerusalem, it happened that he went through the midst of Samaria and Galilee. And as He entered into a certain village, ten leprous men met Him, who stood afar off. And they lifted voice and said, Jesus, Master, pity us! And seeing them, He said to them, Go show yourselves to the priests. And it happened, as they went, that they were cleansed. And one of them, when he saw that he was healed, turned back and glorified God with a loud voice. And he fell down on his face at His feet, thanking Him. And he was a Samaritan. And answering, Jesus said, Were there not ten cleansed? But where are the nine? Were none found who returned to give glory to God except this foreigner? And He said to him, Rise and go; your faith has cured you.

As Jesus entered this village, a group of lepers met Him. As the law demanded, they kept their distance. Leprous people were pronounced "unclean" (Lev 13). Unclean people were deemed sinners and, therefore, lost their entire status. Lepers had to warn people that they had leprosy. They were separated from healthy people and had to live by themselves.

Lev 13:45-46 And as for the leper in whom the plague is, his clothes shall be torn, and his head shall be bare, and he shall put a covering on his upper lip, and shall cry, Unclean! Unclean! All the days in which the plague is in him he shall be defiled. He is unclean. He shall live alone. His dwelling shall be outside the camp.

In July 1986 we as a group undertook a mission trip to Zaire, now known as the Democratic Republic of the Congo. During a few weeks there we built a new building for their little school. On weekends we ministered to the people. One Saturday afternoon we were scheduled to visit a leper colony. Whenever our group visited neighboring villages, the hospital, or presented programs elsewhere, there was always a group of local people who tagged along. On this occasion, however, nobody gathered with us as we were getting ready to go. In fact, not even our translator showed up. We had to find her before we could leave. This showed clearly that the local society did not want to go to the leper colony. Eventually only we and the translator left. We walked down the hill to the leper colony. The colony was about half way between the mission station and the fast flowing river at the bottom of the hill.

Once we got there we had to make a ninety degrees turn to the left. The leper village was about 50 yards from the road. There was a large clearing with a couple of trees in the middle of the bare patch. In the middle of the clearing was the church underneath these trees; it was built from mud bricks and the walls were only waist high. Poles were built into the wall a few feet apart for the roof; the roof was made of palm leaves. At the end of the clearing, away from the road were the little square mud huts. Palm trees towered over the huts.

As we turned left into the clearing a large group of enthusiastic lepers came towards us. Our group and the leprous group started to walk closer to each other: Then they stopped. It was as if there was an invisible "glass wall", preventing them to come closer. We moved closer, but then they moved backwards, maintaining their distance. It was not until our leader, Dr. Ian Hartley, beckoned them to come closer that they came, but hesitantly. Subsequently he held out his hand as an invitation to shake hands: One successful hand shake melted the invisible wall, and they came forward to shake our hands. One could see the longing in their eyes for acceptance: Being touched by a healthy person was the ultimate prize.

New Testament lepers had the same longing. Instead of being looked upon as sinful outcasts they longed for dignity. Jesus understood their need for healing. He knew that they required more than physical healing, they wanted to be restored in society. Jesus demonstrated His acceptance by touching a leper, as previously discussed. He sent this leper to the priest in order for him to be declared clean.

Matt 8:3   And Jesus put out His hand and touched him, saying, I will; be clean! And immediately his leprosy was cleansed.

Since the ten lepers stood far off in this case, Jesus was not able to touch them. Yet, His instruction for them to go to the priest indicated that He did not just want to heal them physically, but that He also wanted to restore them fully. On the way to the priest one of them realizing that he was healed turned around and came back to Jesus. It is important to note that the thankful leper gave glory to God. He then thanked Jesus. It was here where this New Testament story did not seem to make sense to the western mind: Jesus basically asked why the other nine did not also return. Jesus' question corresponded with the leper's actions, for Jesus asked why the other nine did not give glory to God. Please note that Jesus was not asking why they were not thanking Him, but why they were not giving glory to God.

The modern reader might have looked at this story without realizing that which did not make sense to us who were removed from the New Testament times and culture. We might think that it made sense for Jesus to ask this question. We may also consider the other nine to be rude and unthankful for not coming back to express thankfulness. These conclusions were drawn, however, because such "un-thankfulness" would be rude in our culture. When we looked at this story in isolation from the rest of the New Testament and from the perspective of the western mind it would seem to make sense; but if we look at this story in the light of the rest of the New Testament something is missing to understand the narrative correctly.

We have already established that Jesus performed thousands of miracles, and that most of them were healings. Many of these healings were recorded in the New Testament. The question is, other than this lone leper, how many other people did we read about who thanked Jesus after they had been healed? Jesus gave sight to the blind, speech to the dumb and hearing to the deaf; He fed thousands of people and He even raised people from the dead. Yet, only this leper thanked Him. Were all the other New Testament people ungrateful? Surely not! Yet, even stranger, why did Jesus enquire about the other nine, without asking such a question to the thousands who had received miracles previously? It surely seemed that leper was the exception and not the other nine. Usually one would query the exception, not those who acted normally. Since no one else thanked benefactors in the New Testament, should the question not have been, why did this leper thank Jesus? It seemed normal not to express appreciation as nobody else did it in this society.

There were many examples of people thanking God in the Gospels, but there was not one example of a person expressing thanks in the Gospels other than this one leper. In the remainder of the New Testament there was certainly a "theology of thankfulness". This theology also reflected thankfulness to God, however, not towards people. People showed thankfulness to people, however, by thanking God, not to the individual involved. The only verse that seemed to be an exception is in the book of Romans:

Rom 16:4 who have laid down their own necks for my life; to whom not only I give thanks, but also the churches of the nations.

Even here it might be argued that Paul gave thanks to Priscilla and Aquila by thanking God. At the very least, expressing thanks is not to them directly. So, what is going on in the story of the ten lepers? This narrative can only be understood once the New Testament concept of "thankfulness" is understood.

To recap, in the New Testament, social status was determined by those who were willing to associate with certain other people. Even conducting business was considered a form of association. Being associated with people of a higher status than one's own resulted in honor gained. Being associated with people of lower status than one's own resulted in honor lost. People with higher honor had no reason to associate with people from lower ranks because if they did they would lose honor. To associate with higher-ranked people attracting the best deals would be offered to higher-ranked people and they would be assisted first. In a sense the lower-ranked person's good deal was an attempt to buy honor. Lower-ranking people wished to buy goods from higher-ranking people to gain honor, but might have been rejected, required to pay more, and be assisted lastly. This dynamic resulted in groups of the same level of honor generally doing business with each other.

Doing business in this environment was very difficult. Certain classes of people controlled certain markets. This meant that people from a certain level only sold goods that that level of persons had access to. If one wished to buy an item which could not be bought from one's own class it had to be bought from a different class. To purchase such items from lower classes would cost honor. Buying the item from higher classes would cost more money and one had to find a higher ranking person willing to sacrifice honor to sell it to a lower-ranked person in the first place. Doing business, therefore, was not just "doing business", it was a social and relational event. To survive one had to build up and protect such relationships.

During the time of the New Testament "thanking a person" meant an end to the relationship; it was actually the opposite of that which was preferable, namely, to protect relationships. A part of this notion still exists today. When a speech is finalized, the speaker often concludes with the words, "thank you". "Thank you" means that the speech is over. Television stations often conclude their weather or news broadcasts with the words, "thank you for joining us". Stores often have a "thank you" note for their customers, posted above the exit door. "Thank you" means that it is over or finished. When one's survival depends on these relationships it just does not make sense to terminate them. That is why New Testament people did not thank other people: In a sense thanking a person was rude as it was a "declaration" that one did not need the other person anymore and it signified an end to the relationship.

A relationship with God is not subject to this "rule" as a human being cannot make an impact on God's honor. God does not lose honor for associating with lower-ranked people – after all, everyone was lower-ranked than God, and God freely associated with everybody. Hence, God might be thanked without it being considered rude.

In all societies goods (commodities and services) are limited[87]. The New Testament people operated with the distinct concept of

---

[87] Hagedorn and Neyrey 1998:20.

"limited goods"[88]. This meant that gain to one was seen as a lost to another. In any economy certain items are scarce. During a time of scarcity some items became rare and at other times different items became scarce. Oil might be scarce this month, but in abundance during the following year, while grain might be in abundance this month, but scarce next month. During times of scarcity people sold goods to people who were the closest to them relationally and, therefore, also closest to them on the status line. If one did not have a close relationship with the salesman the goods would be sold out prior to becoming available to people further down the relationship line. Consequently, people would do all that they could to build and keep relationships robust. Ending a relationship with a "thank you", would rather be careless in this society.

God's "goods", however, were not limited[89] like people's goods were[90]. God did not experience shortages therefore it would be good to thank God. God would never be placed in a position where He had to choose between two people to assist only one of them on account of running out of "goods". God could not have a shortage. Expressing thankfulness to God is therefore necessary.

So, why then was this Samaritan thanking Jesus? He was certainly not saying, "Jesus, I am healed now, I am not planning on getting sick again, so I don't need You anymore, thank You, and good bye!" There could only be one reason why this leper was thanking Jesus: *He recognized Jesus as God!*

Thanking God is proper. Now things began to make sense. The leper gave glory to God, and, in a sense, not to Jesus. He fell on his face at Jesus' feet when he thanked Him, which was also a form of worship, confirming his view of Jesus' divinity. Consequently, this meant that the other nine lepers did not recognize Jesus as God. Thanking Jesus as a human being would terminate the relationship, and that would be foolish

---

[88] This view made a great impact on New Testament societies. It caused people to be hesitant to advance beyond others (Hagedorn and Neyrey 1998:21). This was necessary, as such an advance was seen as their loss, resulting in envy. Envy lead to being ostracized. In a group-oriented society ostracizing was feared. They did everything in their power not to be cut off or to isolate others. Thanking someone was, in a sense, isolating the other person by ending the relationship.

[89] Crook 2006:89, May 1997:204.

[90] Richards 2008:30.

to do. The thankful leper thanked Jesus as a divine Person, and not as a human being; thus, also not ending the relationship. *Jesus was God.*

☙ CHAPTER FIFTEEN ❧

THE GOOD SAMARITAN[91]

Luke 10:25-37

Like many people this lawyer of Old Testament law also struggled with the assurance of his salvation. On the one hand, he wished to know what he should do to inherit eternal life. His question revealed the theological battle he was waging within himself. The first part of his question involved doing something to gain eternal life. One of the New Testament society's erroneous beliefs was that salvation could be earned by keeping the law. When used in this context the law does not only refer to the Ten Commandments or the Pentateuch, but to all the legalistic laws which the religious leaders instituted. According to this belief salvation was gained as a result of good works, namely, by keeping the law. Hence, his question was about what he should *do*.

On the other hand, his question demonstrated that he also knew that salvation was inherited regardless of good works. Inheritance could

---

[91] Interpretation of this passage differs widely. The allegorization of this story is well documented and dates far back (Roukema 2004). The interpretation employed here leans more heavily on the story's "context". However, some elements of the story will be allegorized for homiletical purposes rather than hermeneutical purposes. It is hoped that the interpretation relates closely to how this story would have been interpreted when it was told. However, in as much as the original context has been recreated to the best of our knowledge it is acknowledged that the original audience's interpretation, although deduced from the context can never be fully known for certain.

be lost due to behavior, but it could not be earned. Inheritance is something you received for being a child, not for what you achieved. He must have struggled with these conflicting ideas. Perhaps he wished to settle the following burning question: Do I gain salvation through what I do or through inheritance? The dichotomy[92] was apparent in the way he put his question: "What must I *do* to *inherit*…"

We also knew that this man's question had not been totally sincere in terms of just wishing to know the answer to his question. His question had ulterior motives. Luke told us quite clearly that this "lawyer" stood up and *tempted* Jesus. Perhaps this suggested that he was not saved, but rather that he was in need of salvation. Perhaps he was being a smart-aleck, a conceited know-it-all, outwardly, but inwardly he wished to be saved. No one could know for sure what was going on in this man's heart, but we do know that his question was interpreted by the author as being a temptation rather than an honest enquiry.

The language used here did suggest that a debate about honor was taking place[93]. We had an educated lawyer addressing Jesus as "Master": That set the stage for two equals to debate the issue. Jesus' answered with a question and that confirmed what was going on here. A New Testament lawyer was someone who was an expert in Old Testament law, in other words, the first five books of the Old Testament. The concept "lawyer" was not to be confused with modern day attorneys. The lawyer's answer demonstrated his knowledge of the Torah, for he quotes Deuteronomy 6:5. Remember that the purpose of the debate was not just to win the debate, but to gain the loser's honor. Honor was bestowed and recognized by the crowd who witnessed the debate. The lawyer's quotation of Scripture, although common in New Testament times, served a further twofold purpose: Firstly, it provided authority to his answer. His answer was supported by the Holy Scriptures. Secondly, he was demonstrating his expertise to the onlookers in an attempt to lure them over to grant him the victory. This debate was as much a debate as it was a show to persuade the crowd to support his "victory".

---

[92] Graves 1997:272.
[93] Richards 2008:31.

Luke 10:27 And answering, he said, You shall love the Lord your God with all your heart, and with all your soul, and with all your strength, and with all your mind, and your neighbor as yourself.

Deut 6:5 And you shall love Jehovah your God with all your heart and with all your soul and with all your might.

He answered the way Jesus wanted him to answer, and that meant, however, that Jesus won the debate. Not ready to concede the victory he asked another question[94]. Luke, who knew the culture of these honor and shame debates, had no problem identifying what was happening here. Luke declared that the man had asked the follow up question to "justify himself". Cleverly he also moved the debate more directly into his field of expertise and thereby providing himself a better chance to win the debate. So, he has asked: "Who is my neighbor?" These lawyers were called upon to interpret the Scriptures, to define what the Bible meant when it mentioned something, and to settle disputes between people with regard to the meaning of the Scriptures. The lawyer's question required a definition of the concept "neighbor". As we already saw, that question was rather loaded. The problem was that an established interpretation on the matter already existed. In fact, there were laws governing the issue who would be considered to be a neighbor and who would not be considered to be a neighbor. In addition, there were laws governing interaction between "neighbors" and "non-neighbors". Everybody knew that the "definition" of the concept, "neighbor", excluded Samaritans[95]. The lawyer was asking the question, however, because by asking this particular question he was positioning himself favorably to win the debate. After all, he was the expert on such matters and was well practiced[96] in this subject matter, while Jesus was not necessarily considered by the public to be an expert in this area. Before Jesus even answered the question the crowd must have leaned towards granting the lawyer victory.

---

[94] This exchange was a classical challenge and response communication as part of an honor and shame debate (Esler 2000:333. Also see Malina 1993:34-37).
[95] Gourgues 1998:713.
[96] Esler 2000:335.

This battle was probably considered no different from modern day people being asked which team was going to win when a high school team would play against a National Football League team. We would expect the National team to win.

It is important to remember that this question has been only a sub-question of the original question on salvation. So when Jesus answered with a parable He was addressing the question, who is my neighbor, as well as, how am I to be saved. Before the actual parable would be discussed this new sub-question would need to be explored further.

New Testament Jewish people believed that they were eligible and entitled for salvation because they were Jews. Non-Jews were considered to be pagan gentiles. These non-Jews were looked down upon, so much so that it was not considered to be a lie when one was not telling them the truth as they did not deserve the truth. Jews would not associate with or have anything to do with non-Jews if they could help it. Non-Jews were even considered to be "unclean". Peter's vision in Acts about the sheet of "unclean" animals was precisely about this issue, it was not about "clean or unclean" food, it was not to regard people as "unclean".

Act 10:28 And he said to them, You know that it is an unlawful thing for a man, a Jew to keep company with or to come near to one of another nation. But God has shown me not to call any man common or unclean. (Also see Acts 11)

This lawyer wanted to limit his liability.[97] He was willing to love his neighbor as himself as long as the neighbor was a Jew, free of disabilities, and from his own status group or preferably higher. Perhaps some public incident had happened between himself and some wretched sinner. His first answer to Jesus might have disputed his action towards this sinner and thus shown him to be in contradiction to his own answer. To save face he had to limit his liability of loving others to exclude certain groups. Of course we did not know whether such an event took place or not, but we knew that he wished to define the word "neighbor" to be applicable to the smallest group possible. It is highly likely,

---

[97] Esler 2000:335-336.

however, that such an event did take place because Luke told us that he wished to "justify himself". One had to ask the question, justifying himself from what. We might not know what happened, but something had happened. Jesus now answered...

> *Luke 10:30   And answering, Jesus said, A certain man went down from Jerusalem to Jericho and fell among robbers, who stripped him of his clothing and wounded him, and departed, leaving him half dead.*

From the perspective of the robbers the term "neighbor" excluded people outside their own group. They probably robbed this man as he was not considered to be a neighbor. "Non-neighbors" were regarded as "legitimate" targets.[98] To someone who also thought that the definition of "neighbor" should be limited as narrowly as possible to avoid duty, the story did not start well, for Jesus equated such people with robbers. Perhaps the emerging message thus far was that limiting the concept of "neighbor" resulted in robbing people from that which was due to them.

Was it by accident or design that Jesus' story was so remarkably similar to this situation before us? A lawyer who stood before Jesus and wanted to know how to be saved, probably because he might have been lost; but he was tempting Jesus and wished to justify himself. Yet, Jesus placed a man in need of "salvation" before the lawyer because if he would not be "saved" he might have died. It was also interesting that many rich lawyers had homes in Jericho.[99] After working for some time in Jerusalem they would depart for Jericho. The victim in Jesus' story was left without an identity. Jesus began the story deliberately by stripping the victim of any identity.[100] Jesus did this by the vague introduction of "a certain man". When Jesus uttered these words the lawyer probably thought that the victim was an Israelite. Secondly, he was left naked so that no one could identify him, whether he was a

---

[98]   Ateek 2008:162.
[99]   Knowles 2004:152. Knowles also referred to the research of Netzer to substantiate this claim. An academic search on Netzer indicated extensive publication on the city of Jericho and particularly with reference to archeological findings in Jericho.
[100]   Esler 2000:337.

Roman, a Samaritan, a Jew, or even someone else.[101] Was Jesus telling the lawyer a story about himself? Was the lawyer the one in need of help? Was he the naked one who would die if he was not saved? The story that Jesus narrated here was perhaps not just a parable, it might have really happened.[102] Yet, it seemed as if Jesus was using it as a parallel to, or metaphor involving, the lawyer himself. Jesus appeared to be applying this physical event to the lawyer's spiritual situation. This narrative was actually the story of salvation. Since that was the very topic of the lawyer's question and since the lawyer asked the question for himself, "What must *I* do...", Jesus was telling him how salvation worked for him. The lawyer was actually inserted in as well as assigned a role in this story-event.

When possible, Jesus had the habit to address people in such a way that their identities were kept secret, and not to embarrass them. When Jesus wished to address the accusers of the woman, caught in adultery, He did so by writing in the sand. Each accuser could identify his own sin without the crowd's knowledge.

> *John 8:6-9 They said this, tempting Him so that they might have reason to accuse Him. But bending down, Jesus wrote on the ground with His finger, not appearing to hear. But as they continued to ask Him, He lifted Himself up and said to them, He who is without sin among you; let him cast the first stone at her. And again bending down, He wrote on the ground. And hearing, and being convicted by conscience, they went out one by one, beginning at the oldest, until the last. And Jesus was left alone, and the woman standing in the midst.*

Perhaps Jesus was doing the same thing here in Luke's narrative. He was telling the lawyer a story not only to answer his question, but also to answer a much deeper need, the need to be saved. In other words, this was not just a theological debate about some trivial question of contention, but it was rather a personal question asked by a lost man who wished to veil the question so as not to lose status by declaring publically that he was the one who was lost. The fact that the victim in the story was left naked, directly answered the question, who qualified as

---

[101] Bailey 1980:42-43.
[102] Desire of Ages, 499.

a neighbor, as he was not identifiable. How was someone going to decide to love and care for him; how would someone decide whether he was a neighbor or not if he was not identifiable? Yet, he might very well have died if someone did not reject the typical New Testament Jewish understanding of a very narrow liability.

There might have been also another reason why Jesus' story was designed in such a way as to leave the victim unidentifiable. This way the man was stripped not only of his clothing, but also of his identity. In other words, his identity as a Jew was taken away.[103] What Jesus taught the lawyer was firstly, that he was wounded and in need of salvation, and secondly, that being a Jew did not assist him to be saved. The wounded man was without identity and actually unidentifiable to people coming his way. Ethnic identity was disregarded by the Savior. At the very least, the one who saved him would not do this on account of the victim being a Jew. Jesus had broken down the lawyer's preconceived ideas about who and how someone would inherit eternal life, as well as what would constitute a neighbor.

Furthermore, clothing was a strong indicator of status[104]. Luke specifically and regularly mentioned clothing as a status symbol. Examples of such texts are the following:

Luke 7:25 But what did you go out to see? A man clothed with soft clothing? Behold, those in splendid clothing and being in luxury are in kings' palaces.

Luke 16:19 There was a certain rich man who was customarily clothed in purple and fine linen and making merry in luxury every day.

Luke 15:22 But the father said to his servants, Bring the best robe and put it on him. And put a ring on his hand and shoes on his feet.

---

[103] Samaritans were also circumcised. Even though the robbed man was left naked, thereby exposing the fact of circumcision or the lack of circumcision, it still did not resolve the problem whether or not this man was a neighbor, a Jew, or a "non-neighbor", a Samaritan. So, whether the victim was circumcised or not, this would still not reveal his identity. Now, if the man was not circumcised he would not have been deemed to be a neighbor and would have been classified as a pagan.

[104] Knowles 2004:156.

Luke 20:46 Beware of the scribes who desire to walk in long robes, and love greetings in the markets, and the first seats in the synagogues, and the chief places at the feasts;

Acts 12:21 And on a certain day, Herod sat on his throne, dressed in royal clothing, and made a speech to them[105].

In addition, it was rather significant that the victim was stripped naked, as it stripped the victim of any indication of status. Status played a pivotal role in in-group/out-group identity. In other words, status was one of the tools used to ascertain whether or not someone could be seen as a neighbor. The victim was truly unidentifiable; every indication that could have been used to determine his identity was taken away. The statement was clear: Salvation was not granted on the basis of earthly status that was also stripped away. Not only was the indication of status stripped away, but also being without clothing was humiliating. Being undressed by others was even worse. This man's status by way of the act of stripping became unacceptable. Being undressed was an act of becoming a real sinner. He now fell below the unacceptable horizontal line on the vertical status line.[106] To many he would not be seen as a neighbor due to his lack of any status. Jesus was creating a remarkable contrast here with the use of clothing. On the one hand, the priest, the Levite and the Samaritan[107] would have been clothed in distinctive attire;[108] on the other hand, the wounded man was left naked.

Notice also how Jesus set up an expectation and how that expectation was fulfilled. Everyone knew that the road between Jerusalem and Jericho was a dangerous road. It wound through a

---

[105] Luke was also the author of the book of Acts. Scholars widely accepted this point. In fact, in the opening verse of Acts reference was made of the book, the Gospel of Luke.

[106] Nakedness was associated with profound shame. For further reading regarding this topic see the work of Hamel, 1990:73-75.

[107] Knowles had a long discussion about the dress codes which applied to the Samaritans. They too wore distinctive clothing (Knowles 2004:164-168). It should also be noted that both Josephus and Philo also contained information with regard to clothing and status. In fact, it was reported that certain groups actually applied to Roman authorities for permission to be allowed to wear certain items which denoted status and/or position.

[108] Knowles 2004:158.

mountainous, rocky part of the country, which made it ideal for bandits to live, hide and rob people. Jesus set up the possibility of a robbery by citing a dangerous road. Now Jesus set up a second expectation:

Luke 10:31 And by coincidence a certain priest came down that way and seeing him, he passed by on the opposite side.

In our culture we would expect the priest would to stop and assist the wounded man. He would be judged to be a terrible priest if he would not comply with our expectation, but in New Testament times this priest did exactly what the audience of this story would have expected him to do. Priests worked in the temple. Numbers 19 clearly stated that anyone who touched a dead body would be unclean for seven days. Thus the priest faced a dilemma. On the one hand, his human empathy would urge him to stop and assist the victim.[109] On the other hand, the priest knew that if the victim would die on the way to the city, he would be rendered unclean.[110] If he was unclean he would not be able to perform his duties in the temple (Leviticus 21:1-4, 11). If he could not perform his duties in the temple, the sins of those who came to sacrifice would not be forgiven. His duty as a priest would urge him to keep on going. In a group-oriented society the group always came before the individual. The New Testament Jewish hearer knew these things and agreed with them. Thus, when Jesus mentioned a priest the expectation was for the priest not to stop and assist. The expectation was fulfilled as the priest walked by. In fact, he would be regarded as a good priest as he was willing to sacrifice the individual for the benefit of the group. He even took precautions not to accidentally touch the victim by walking around him. The New Testament listeners of the story probably wanted to give this priest a raise. He was a trustworthy priest who put the nation before the individual. He could be counted on as a priest; he was faithful to the priesthood.

If a priest's job description would be generalized it could be summed up with one word, intercession. It was the priest's job to intercede between the people and God. The priest was the one who went into the sanctuary on behalf of the sinner to face God. Jesus was

---

[109] Bauckham 1998:477-478.
[110] Gourgues 1998:79.

telling the lawyer that he was in need of salvation for fear that he died. Being a Jew would not save him, and now Jesus went on to state that neither the priest would save him. No other human being could have interceded for him. In fact, they did not even come close to him as they walked by on the other side!

Luke 10:32 And in the same way a Levite, also being at the place, coming and seeing him, he passed on the opposite side.

Levites were special people too. They were also instructed by the same rules as the priests, and neither would the Levite assist him. Once again, Jesus' point was not that we were dealing with corrupt and bad priests and Levites here. They behaved in the exactly the manner in which the New Testament audience would have expected them to do. Levites were the teachers in the synagogues. They cleaned the temple and the temple implements. They also served as the treasurers of the synagogues and the temple. In a sense they were the administrators of the church. They ran the synagogues. If this Levite would assist the robbed man and the man would die on the way he would have been declared unclean, just like the priest would have been. If the Levite was unclean he would not have been able to clean the temple implements. If the temple implements were not cleaned the priests could not intercede. If the priests could not intercede the people's sins would not be forgiven. Once again, this Levite placed the needs of the group before that of the individual. The New Testament Jewish listeners to this story would have felt very positive towards the Levite. The Levite represented the church, the institution of their religion.

Jesus was also telling the lawyer that the institution of the church could not save him. In fact, the church, in this case its representative, the Levite, did not even come close by, the "church" walked by the other side. So, how would the picture of this lawyer look as portrayed in Jesus' parable? He thought that he had it made because he was a Jew; he thought he had it made because of his faithful participation in rituals where the priests interceded for him. He thought he had it made because he was a lawyer for the institution of the "church". Jesus, however, told him that he was in dire need of salvation. The fact that he was a Jew was stripped away, the priest's intercession was removed, and the church as institution could not save him. By now he must have been wondering desperately: If not by my Jewish heritage, if not by the priestly intercession, if not by the institution of the church, then by whom or how could he be saved? Jesus continued...

Luke 10:33 But a certain traveling Samaritan came upon him, and seeing him, he was filled with pity.

Thus far Jesus' parable had created a number of expectations and all were fulfilled, but now, what happened here must have shocked the New Testament audience. The notion of a Samaritan arriving on the scene of the desperately wounded man probably provoked thoughts of ill reputation. They must have thought the worst; surely the Samaritan would spit on the robbed man. Samaritans were hated by the Jews.[111] It was a good thing that the victim was unconscious, because if he was not, he would have refused help from the Samaritan. He would rather have chosen to die instead of being assisted by a Samaritan.

Jesus chose a Samaritan as the "savior" for a definite purpose. If the lawyer would be saved because he was a Jew, he would have deserved it by virtue of his race. If the priest or the Levite would have saved him he could also have argued that his salvation was deserved as they were just returning the favor; he served the church and now they served him in return. A Samaritan, however, had no reason to save him. As far as the Samaritan was concerned the victim did not deserve salvation because of who he was, or what he had done, and because of everything that was unknown: He was an unidentifiable human being in need of help. The Samaritan assisted him because he was filled with pity, and not because of what the victim deserved. *This Samaritan was none other than Jesus.*[112] Jesus was despised just as Samaritans were loathed.

Isa 53:3 He is despised and rejected of men; a Man of sorrows, and acquainted with grief; and as it were a hiding of faces from Him, He being despised, and we esteemed Him not.

---

[111] Resmer 2002:39.
[112] Roukema 2004:57, 72.

Luke 22:37 For I say to you that this which is written must yet be accomplished in Me, "And he was reckoned among the transgressors"; for the things concerning Me have an end.

It is rather interesting that the Jews once accused Jesus of being a Samaritan; perhaps these were prophetic words…

John 8:48 Then the Jews answered and said to Him, Do we not say well that you are a Samaritan and have a demon?

The lawyer was taught that salvation was possible because of what went on in Jesus' heart. Oh, when Satan leaves us bleeding, broken and wounded by the way side, know that Jesus is coming that way! When Jesus saw us His heart was filled with compassion. Jesus did not think, "I wondered what he or she has done this time …", instead Jesus was filled with compassion and He leaped into action.

Luke 10:34 And coming near, he bound up his wounds, pouring on oil and wine, and set him on his own animal and brought him to an inn, and took care of him.

Jesus knelt down and tended to the lawyer. This was so typical of Jesus: He tended even to those who tempted Him, and those who wished to justify themselves at His expense. Perhaps that was the precise point: The lawyer did not deserve being treated well since he was not willing to acknowledge his mistakes. Justifying himself implied that he did not even know that he was wounded and dying, or at the very least, he was not willing to admit it. He was not willing to believe that he had a problem, yet he was not quite sure. Something was bugging him because he wished to know what he must do to be saved. The difference between his view of himself and Jesus' view of him was that his question implied that he thought he could do something to be saved, while Jesus' story implied that he could not do anything to be saved: He was "half dead" and left for "dead".

One had to ask with what did the "Samaritan" bind up the "lawyer's" wounds? It was not likely that "he" happened to be carrying a load of bandages with him just in case "he" needed them. Even if "he" had a little emergency kit at hand it would hardly suffice as the "lawyer" was beaten up so badly that he was left for dead. The Greek words used for the assault clearly implies that the victim was continuously pounded. These wounds would represent more than just a few little gashes. In all likelihood the Samaritan had to use his own clothing to bind up the victim's wounds. Where else would he get enough cloths for this purpose? Being dressed by a benefactor was certainly indicated by Jesus as having salvific implications.

> *Luke 15:22-24 But the father said to his servants, Bring the best robe and put it on him. And put a ring on his hand and shoes on his feet. And bring the fattened calf here and kill it. And let us eat and be merry, for this my son was dead and is alive again, he was lost and is found. And they began to be merry.*

> *Matt 22:11-12 And the king coming in to look over the guests, he saw a man there who did not have on a wedding garment. And he said to him, Friend, how did you come in here without having a wedding garment? And he was speechless.*

We are saved because Jesus covered our wounds with his cloak of righteousness. In Matthew 22 access was gained to the King's wedding celebration by wearing the King's wedding garment. Someone was expelled because he was not wearing the King's garment; he probably thought that his garment was good enough.

Not only did "Jesus" bind up his wounds with his own garments, but he also poured oil and wine onto the injuries. Samaria was well known for its oil and wine during this time of the year. Perhaps the Samaritan was an oil and wine merchant. This deduction is based on the fact that he had the items at hand, and he was traveling with a packed animal on a planned route since he told the innkeeper later that he would return, and that he was on his way to Jericho; the place where aristocrats lived and where there was a market for oil and wine.[113] Both oil and wine had various uses, both physically and metaphorically. The oil could very well represent consecration and dedication, while the wine could refer to Jesus' blood. After being treated the "lawyer" was placed on the

---

[113] Knowles 2004:151-152, 154.

"Samaritan's" donkey. The donkey's role was to transport this injured man to the inn. He did so while walking with the Samaritan, "Jesus".

God had always used people to lead or carry others to places of healing and growing. As "donkeys", "beasts of burden", church folk needed to remember that it was still the Samaritan who saved the man and not the donkey. We needed to understand that our role would be to walk with Jesus; He would place those in need on our backs. The load might be heavy and the road might be rocky, steep and winding, but we should never forget the One, who is walking on that same road with us, in fact, next to us. We should never forget that another person's life is at stake. Oh, and please remember that the person on your back is critically injured: Please walk slowly and gently.

We often think that "Jesus" just dropped the "lawyer" off at the inn and rode off into sunset. Yet, the text clearly stated that He "brought him to an inn, and took care of him". "Jesus" did not leave until the next day. "He" continued to care for the "lawyer". Now an interesting development took place in a remarkable display of trust and responsibility.

Luke 10:35 And going on the next day, he took out two denarii and gave them to the innkeeper, and said to him, Take care of him. And whatever more you spend, when I come again I will repay you.

"Jesus" left the victim in the care of the innkeeper; He also paid him for the initial expense. What is more remarkable is that Jesus offered to repay all future expenses without limit. The inn was a place of safety where this man could heal.

God wanted hurting people to be brought to the church for healing and growth. The church contained both healing and growing people, as well as "innkeepers", whose job it would be to care for the injured. We often would not wish to spend money on the injured, thinking that it would be money lost. Jesus, however, promised to refund "whatever is spent" when He would come again. We would need to be willing to spend whatever it took to get a victim healed. Jesus did not place any limits on how much He was willing to refund. That ought to teach us how much Jesus valued people.

This contract was full of trust[114] and responsibility. There was not much biblical or extra-biblical data on innkeepers.[115] It could safely be concluded that innkeepers were mostly of ill repute.[116] Why would the Samaritan trust the innkeeper? "Jesus" was trusting that the innkeeper would care for the victim. The innkeeper could easily have waited for "Jesus" to leave the next day, pocketed the two denarii and kicked out the "lawyer". "Jesus" placed the responsibility of this man's wellbeing on the innkeepers' shoulders. Yet, the innkeeper was also expected to place an enormous amount of trust in "Jesus". After all, he was required to spend *whatever* it took to heal this man in the hope and trust that the Samaritan would in fact return and refund the money spent as promised. The trust was mutual and reciprocal. Just as Jesus reversed the Samaritan's role from being a worthless sinner to being a hero, He also turned the innkeeper's usual reputation from distrusted keeper to trustworthy keeper. Jesus was building the case that the outcasts were their true neighbors.

Then Jesus' counter question was posed to the lawyer …

Luke 10:36 Then which of these three, do you think, was neighbor to him who fell among the robbers?

It was mentioned that this story possibly referred to an actual event, but it was also surmised that Jesus used this story deliberately with reference to the lawyer's actual situation. Here Jesus' counter question provided some evidence of Jesus' intent to use this story as a way to talk directly to the lawyer about his situation without the crowd realizing this man's embarrassment. The lawyer originally asked, "Who is my neighbor"? In other words, to whom am I limited to, to show love and kindness? He thought of himself as the one who was showing the love and kindness. His view was that someone else was in need of him as the benefactor. Jesus' counter question here, however, clearly reversed that view:[117] Jesus did not ask, "Who is *my* neighbor", or in other words,

---

[114] Longenecker 2009:436, 440.
[115] Longenecker 2009:430.
[116] Longenecker 2009:431-433.
[117] Resmer 2002:38.

"Who was *I* a neighbor to?"[118] Instead of asking what this man thought *he* wanted to know, Jesus asked, "*who* was the neighbor?", or "who was the neighbor *to me?*"[119]

To begin with, the lawyer viewed himself in the role of the Samaritan, the person assisting others; and not in the person of the Samaritan, for Samaritans were classified as sinners; but Jesus viewed him as the half dead sufferer. Jesus did not view the lawyer as the Samaritan because He followed his narrative by saying: "Go and do likewise." This implied that he was not currently doing so.

Luke 10:37 And he said, The one doing the deed of mercy to him. And Jesus said to him, Go and do likewise.

The lawyer's answer demonstrated just how strong the stereotyped view of Samaritans was. He knew that he was required by logic to answer, "the Samaritan", but he could not even bring himself to utter the word.[120] So, instead he answers: "The one doing the deed of mercy."

Jesus' closing remark in verse 37 was for all who did not understand what Jesus said. Jesus wished to make sure that no one misunderstood Him. He knew that most of the audience listening to this encounter also believed that their liability towards others was very limited and applied only to certain groups. Jesus did not want that conviction to continue. Consequently, what Jesus said here was the following: "Mr. Lawyer, you are half dead and in need of salvation. You can only be saved by Me. Oh, and by the way, no, your liability towards others is not limited." This last statement is so similar to Jesus' message to the woman caught in adultery, where Jesus said: "I do not judge you, there is forgiveness, but I am not excusing what you did, go and sin no more."

---

[118] Longenecker 2009:423.
[119] Gourgues 1998:713; Fitzmyer 1985:884.
[120] Esler 2000:344.

THE END

Pierre F. Steenberg, Ph.D., D.Min.

❧ CHAPTER SIXTEEN ❧

BIBLIOGRAPHY

Ateek, N   2008   "Who Is My Neighbor?" *Interpretation* 62, no. 2:156-165.

Bailey, K E   1980   *Through Peasant Eyes: More Lucan Parables, their Culture and Style.* Grand Rapids: W. B. Eerdmans Pub. Co.

Bauckham, R 1998   "The Scrupulous Priest and the Good Samaritan: Jesus' Parabolic Interpretation of the Law of Moses." *New Testament Studies* 44:475-489.

Campbell, B L   1995   *Honor, Shame, and the Rhetoric of 1 Peter.* PhD diss., Fuller Theological Seminary.

--   2005 "Honor, Hospitality and Haughtiness: the Contention for Leadership in 3 John. "*Evangelical Quarterly* 77, no. 4, Oct: 321-341.

Chance, J K 1994   "The Anthropology of Honor and Shame: Culture, Values, and Practice." *Semeia* no. 68, Jan. 1:139-151.

Crook, Z A 2006   "Method and Models in New Testament Interpretation: A Critical Engagement with Louise Lawrence's

Literary Ethnography." *Religious Studies Review* 32, no. 2, Apr. 1:87-97.

DeSilva, D A 1996 "The Wisdom of Ben Sira: Honor, Shame, and the Maintenance of the Values of a Minority Culture." *Catholic Biblical Quarterly* 58, no. 3, July:433.

Dixon, M C 1989 *Discipleship in 1 Peter as a Model for Contextual Mission.* PhD diss: The Southern Baptist Theological Seminary.

Downing, F G 1999 "'Honor' among Exegetes." *Catholic Biblical Quarterly* 61, no. 1, Jan. 1:53-73.

Driggers, I B 2007 "The Politics of Divine Presence: Temple as Locus of Conflict in the Gospel of Mark." *Biblical Interpretation* 15, no. 3:227-247.

Esler, P F 1994 *The First Christians in Their Social Worlds: Social-Scientific Approaches to New Testament Interpretation.* 1st ed. New York: Routledge.

-- 2000 "Jesus and the Reduction of Intergroup Conflict: The Parable of the Good Samaritan in the Light of Social Identity Theory." *Biblical Interpretation* 8, no. 4, Oct:325-357.

Fitzmyer, J A 1985 *The Gospel According to Luke X-XXIV (The Anchor Yale Bible Commentaries).* New Haven: Yale University Press.

Friedrichsen, T A 2005 "The Temple, a Pharisee, a Tax Collector, and the Kingdom of God: Rereading a Jesus Parable (Luke 18:10-14A)." *Journal of Biblical Literature* 124, no. 1, Spring:89-119.

Goranson, S 1990 "Pharisees, Sadducees, Essenes, and 4QMMT." In *Biblical Archaeologist* 53, no. 2, June 1:70-71.

Gourgues, M 1998 "The Priest, the Levite, and the Samaritan Revisited: A Critical Note on Luke 10:31-35." *Journal of Biblical Literature* 117, no. 4, Dec. 1:709-713.

Graves, M   1997   "Luke 10:25-37 : "The Moral of the 'Good Samaritan' Story?." *Review & Expositor* 94, no. 2, March 1:269-275.

Hagedorn, A C & Neyrey J H   1998   "'It Was Out of Envy that They Handed Jesus Over' (Mark 15:10) : The Anatomy of Envy and the Gospel of Mark." *Journal for the Study of the New Testament* 69:15-56.

Hamel, G H 1990   *Poverty and Charity in Roman Palestine First Three Centuries C.E. (University of California Publications Near Eastern Studies).* Berkeley: University of California Press.

Haskell, R   2008   "Matthew   17:24-27:   A   Religio-Political Reading." *Evangelical Review of Theology.* Apr 1, 32:173-184.

Hellerman, J H   2000   "Challenging the Authority of Jesus: Mark 11:27-33 and Mediterranean Notions of Honor and Shame." *Journal of the Evangelical Theological Society* 43, no. 2: 213-228.

Kanter, Rabbi Shamai 2004 "Pharisees." *First Things: A Monthly Journal of Religion & Public Life* no. 144, June 6.

Keener, C S   2005   "'Brood   of   Vipers'   (Matt.   3:7;   12:34; 23.33)." *Journal for the Study of the New Testament* 28, no. 1, September:3-11.

Knowles, M P 2004   "What   Was   the   Victim   Wearing?   Literary, Economic, and Social Contexts for the Parable of the Good Samaritan." *Biblical Interpretation* 12, no. 2:145-174.

Longenecker, B W 2009 "The Story of the Samaritan and the Innkeeper (Luke 10:30-35): A study in Character Rehabilitation." *Biblical Interpretation* 17, no. 4, January 1:422-447.

Lawrence, L   2003   Joy. *Ethnography of the Gospel of Matthew: A Critical Assessment of the Use of the Honour & Shame Model in New Testament Studies (Wissenschaftliche Untersuchungen Zum Neuen Testament 2, 165).* New York: Paul Mohr Verlag.

Malina, B J   1993   *The New Testament World: Insights from Cultural Anthropology*. 2nd ed. Louisville: Westminster John Knox Press.

--   1996   *The Social World of Jesus and the Gospels*. 1st ed. New York: Routledge.

--   2002   The Social-Scientific Methods in Historical Jesus Research. In *The Social Setting of Jesus and the Gospels*, eds. Stegemann W, Malina B J and Theissen G:3-26. Minneapolis: Fortress Press.

--   1991   Malina, B J and Neyrey, J H.   "First-Century Personality: Dyadic, Not Individual." In *The Social World of Luke-Acts: Models for Interpretation*, ed. Neyrey J H:67-96. Peabody, Mass: Hendrickson.

Malina, B J & Neyrey, J H 1996 *Portraits of Paul: An Archaeology of Ancient Personality*. Louisville: Westminster John Knox Press.

Malina, B J & Rohrbaugh R L 2003 *Social-Science Commentary on the Synoptic Gospels*. 2nd ed. Minneapolis: Augsburg Fortress Publishers.

May, D M   1997   "Drawn from Nature or Common Life. Social and Cultural Reading Strategies for the Parables." *Review & Expositor* 94, no. 2, March 1:199-214.

Moessner, D P   1988   "The 'Leaven of the Pharisees' and 'this Generation': Israel's rejection of Jesus according to Luke." *Journal for the Study of the New Testament* no. 34, Oct. 1:21-46.

Moxnes, H   1996   Honor and Shame. In *The Social Sciences and New Testament Interpretation*, ed. Rohrbaugh, R:19-40. Peabody, Mass: Hendrickson Publishers.

Neyrey, J H   1998   *Honor and Shame in the Gospel of Matthew*. 1st ed. Louisville: Westminster John Knox Press.

Oakman, D E 1997   "Book reviews." *Catholic Biblical Quarterly* 59, no. 4, Oct: 787.

Pilch, J J 2002   *Cultural Tools for Interpreting the Good News*. Collegeville, MN: Liturgical Press.

Plutarch 1928   *Moralia, Volume II* (Loeb Classical Library). London: William Heinemann Ltd.

--   1931   *Plutarch: Moralia, Volume III (Loeb Classical Library No. 245)*. London: Loeb Classical Library.

Regev, E 2005   "Were the Priests all the Same? Qumranic Halakhah in Comparison with Sadducean Halakhah." *Dead Sea Discoveries* 12, no. 2:158-188.

--   2006   "The Sadducees, the Pharisees, and the Sacred: Meaning and Ideology in the Halakhic Controversies between the Sadducees and Pharisees." *Review of Rabbinic Judaism* 9, no. 1, June:126-140.

Resmer, A S   2002   "Who is our Neighbor? Preaching on the Good Samaritan." *Living Pulpit* 11, no. 3:38-39.

Richards, E R 2008   "An Honor/Shame Argument for Two Temple Clearings." *Trinity Journal* 29, no. 1:19-43.

Roukema, R 2004   "The Good Samaritan in Ancient Christianity." *Vigiliae Christianae* 58, no. 1 February:56-74.

Saldarini, A J 1988   *Pharisees, Scribes and Sadducees in Palestinian Society: A Sociological Approach*. Wilmington, Delaware: Michael Glazier.

Simmonds, A R   2009   "'Woe to you ... hypocrites!' Re-Reading Matthew 23:13-36." *Bibliotheca sacra* 166, no. 663, Jul. 1:336-349.

Steenberg, P F   2000   *The Reversal of Roles as the Reasoning for Remaining Christian in the Face of Hardship in the First Epistle of Peter*. PhD diss., University of Pretoria, South Africa.

Pierre F. Steenberg, Ph.D., D.Min.

ABOUT THE AUTHOR

Pierre F. Steenberg attained a B.A. Theology degree from Andrews University, Michigan. He also accomplished a B.A. Honors in Biblical Studies, an M.A. in Biblical Studies and a Ph.D. in New Testament Studies from the University of Pretoria in South Africa. Both the M.A. and the Ph.D. were attained with distinction - the highest possible grade presented at a South African University. He graduated more recently *Magna Cum Laude* with a D.Min. in Pastoral Psychology and Family Therapy from the Pacific School of Religion, Berkeley, California. He is a member of numerous academic societies in both theology and counseling, including the Society of Biblical Literature and the American Association of Christian Counselors. He is the author of a number of articles and books.

Pierre has been a pastor and a counselor for many years, enjoying the credentials of the BCCC (Board Certified Christian Counselor) from the International Board of Christian Counselors. He is married to Karlien and they have two sons. The Steenberg family lives in California. Pierre enjoys photography and travel.

Other books by the author:

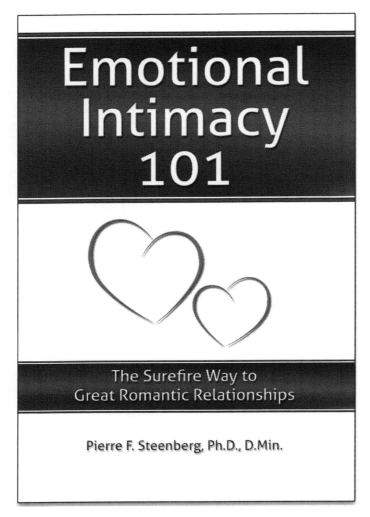

Coming Soon:

Relational Safety 101: The Surefire Way to Secure Romantic Relationships

Relational Commitment 101: The Surefire Way to Lasting Romantic Relationships

Physical Intimacy 101: The Surefire Way to Satisfying Romantic Relationships

64108738R00099

Made in the USA
Lexington, KY
28 May 2017